Securities Regulation

Second Edition

1999 Supplement

Editorial Advisory Board

ASPEN PUBLISHERS, INC.
Legal Education Division

Richard A. Epstein
James Parker Hall Distinguished Service
Professor of Law
University of Chicago

E. Allan Farnsworth
Alfred McCormack Professor of Law
Columbia University

Ronald J. Gilson
Charles J. Meyers Professor of Law and Business
Stanford University
Marc and Eva Stern Professor of Law and Business
Columbia University

Geoffrey C. Hazard, Jr.
Trustee Professor of Law
University of Pennsylvania

James E. Krier
Earl Warren DeLano Professor of Law
University of Michigan

Elizabeth Warren
Leo Gottlieb Professor of Law
Harvard University

Bernard Wolfman
Fessenden Professor of Law
Harvard University

1999 Supplement
Securities Regulation
Cases and Materials
Second Edition

James D. Cox
Professor of Law
Duke University

Robert W. Hillman
Professor of Law
University of California, Davis

Donald C. Langevoort
Professor of Law
Georgetown University

ASPEN LAW & BUSINESS
A Division of Aspen Publishers, Inc.
Gaithersburg   New York

Copyright © 1999 by James D. Cox, Robert W. Hillman, and Donald C. Langevoort

All rights reserved. No part of this publication may be reproduced or transmitted in any form or by any means, electronic or mechanical, including photocopy, recording, or any information storage and retrieval system, without permission in writing from the publisher. Requests for permission to make copies of any part of this publication should be mailed to:

> Permissions
> Aspen Law & Business
> 1185 Avenue of the Americas
> New York, NY 10036

Printed in the United States of America

ISBN 0-7355-0245-5

1 2 3 4 5 6 7 8 9 0

About Aspen Law & Business, Legal Education Division

In 1996, Aspen Law & Business welcomed the Law School Division of Little, Brown and Company into its growing business—already established as a leading provider of practical information to legal practitioners.

Acquiring much more than a presitigious collection of educational publications by the country's foremost authors, Aspen Law & Business inherited the long-standing Little, Brown tradition of excellence—born over 150 years ago. As one of America's oldest and most venerable publishing houses, Little, Brown and Company commenced in a world of change and challenge, innovation and growth. Sharing that same spirit, Aspen Law & Business has dedicated itself to continuing and strengthening the integrity begun so many years ago.

ASPEN LAW & BUSINESS
A Division of Aspen Publishers, Inc.
A Wolters Kluwer Company
<www.aspenpublishers.com>

Table of Contents

Table of Cases   xi

|| 2 ||
Inquiries into the Materiality of Information   1

B. The "Total Mix" of Information and Market Efficiency   1
D. Forward-Looking Information   2
    3. Management Discussion and Analysis   2

|| 3 ||
The Definition of a Security   5

H. Partnership Interests as Securities   5
    Steinhardt Group, Inc. v. Citicorp   5

|| 4 ||
The Public Offering   13

B. Registration Under the '33 Act   13
    4. Preparation and Review of the Registration Statement   13
        c. Plain English Disclosures   13
C. Gun Jumping   18
    2. The Waiting Period   18
        c. Selling Practices During the Waiting Period   18
    4. Reforming the Public Offering Process—The "Aircraft Carrier" Release   19

F.	The International Public Offering	22
	2. Offerings Outside the United States: Regulation S	22

‖ 5 ‖

Exempt Transactions   27

D.	Regulation D and the Limited Offering Exemptions	27
	5. Limitations on the Manner and Scope of an Offering	27
	6. Determining the Aggregate Offering Price in Offerings Under Rules 504 and 505	28
	8. Additional Regulation D Requirements and Features	28
E.	Employee Plans and Contracts Relating to Compensation: Rule 701	28

‖ 6 ‖

Secondary Distributions   31

D.	Rule 144—Safe Harbor for Resales of Control and Restricted Securities	31

‖ 7 ‖

Recapitalizations, Reorganizations, and Acquisitions   33

C.	Reorganizations Under Section 3(a)(10)	33
	1. Nonbankruptcy Reorganizations	33

‖ 8 ‖

Exempt Securities   35

B.	Municipal Securities	35
	6. Rule 15c2-12	35

9

Liability Under the Securities Acts — 37

C. Section 12(a)(2) — 37
   1. By Means of a "Prospectus or Oral Communication" — 37
      Dietrich v. Bauer — 37
      Vannest v. Sage, Rutty & Co., Inc. — 38

11

Fraud in Connection with the Purchase or Sale of a Security — 41

A. What is Proscribed by Rule 10b-5 — 41
   1. Fraud "In Connection With" the Purchase or Sale of a Security — 41
      b. The "In Connection With" Requirement at the Margins — 41
B. Private Rights of Action Under Rule 10b-5 — 42
   2. Pleading Fraud — 42

12

The Regulation of Insider Trading — 45

B. The Source of a Duty to Abstain or Disclose — 45
F. The Misappropriation Theory — 46
      United States v. O'Hagan — 46

13

Shareholder Voting and Going Private Transactions — 61

A. Management Solicitations — 61
   2. Shareholder Proposals — 61

14

Corporate Takeovers — 63

B. The Early Warning System: Section 13(d) — 63
C. Tender Offer Regulation: Controlling the Bidder — 63

‖ 15 ‖

The Enforcement of the Securities Laws 67

C.	More on the Private Enforcement of the Securities Laws		67
	1.	Champion of the Little Guy: The Class Action	67
	5.	Secondary Liability	68
		a. Aiding and Abetting	68
		Wright v. Ernst & Young LLP	69
D.	The Duties of the Securities Lawyer		73
E.	The SEC's Power to Discipline Professionals		74

‖ 16 ‖

Regulation of the Securities Markets and Securities Professionals 77

A.	The Structure of Regulation and the Evolution of the Securities Markets		77
	Exchange Act Release No. 38672		77
C.	The Responsibility of Brokers to their Customers		89
	3.	Suitability	89
		Banca Cremi, S.A. v. Alex. Brown & Sons, Inc.	90
	5.	Price Protection: Markups and Other Matters	94

‖ 17 ‖

The Investment Advisers and Investment Company Act of 1940 95

B.	Mutual Funds and Other Investment Companies		95
	3.	Sales and Redemptions of Mutual Fund Shares	95
		b. Sales Literature and Advertising	95

‖ 18 ‖

Transnational Securities Fraud 97

A.	The Extraterritorial Application of U.S. Securities Laws		97
	1.	In General	97
		Kauthar SDN BHD v. Sternberg	97
	3.	Jurisdiction Based in Whole, or in Part, upon Conduct	103
		Europe and Overseas Commodity Traders, S.A., v. Banque Paribas London	103

Table of Cases

Italics indicate principal cases. All references are to casebook pages.

Baesa Securities Litigation, In re, 741

Banca Cremi, S.A. v. Alex. Brown & Sons, Inc., 1105, 1120

Checkosy v. SEC, 1062

Dietrich v. Bauer, 634

Eisenstadt v. Centel Corp., 62

Epstein v. MCA, Inc., 977

Europe and Overseas Commodity Traders, S.A., v. Banque Paribas London, 334, 1216

Kauthar SDN BHD v. Sternberg, 1204

Press v. Chemical Investment Services Corp., 690

Rehm v. Eagle Financial Corp., 741

S.E.C. v. Fehn, 1057

S.E.C. v. Jakubowski, 690

Silicon Graphics Securities Litigation, In re., 741

Steinhardt Group, Inc. v. Citicorp, 179

United States v. Adler, 782

United States v. O'Hagan, 800

United States v. Smith, 782

Vannest v. Sage, Rutty & Co., Inc., 634

Wright v. Ernst & Young LLP, 1019

2

Inquiries into the Materiality of Information

B. The "Total Mix" of Information and Market Efficiency

Page 62. Add the following new material after the carryover paragraph and before the Problem.

    3. Puffery.   *Eisenstadt v. Centel Corp.*,113 F.3d 738 (7th Cir. 1997), provides an interesting analysis of puffery. Centel Corporation announced it had retained two investment banking firms to assist it in orchestrating its sale through a competitive auction. Following the announcement, the stock quickly rose to $48 per share (from $37). In the ensuing weeks, Centel and its investment bankers were repeatedly disappointed as one prospective bidder after another informed them they were not interested in purchasing Centel. Despite such private bad news, Centel publicly exuded an optimistic image through repeated press announcements that the auction process was going smoothly. Ultimately Centel received only seven disappointingly low bids. It rejected all seven and negotiated its sale $33.50 per share to a nonbidder. A class action was initiated on behalf of those who purchased in reliance upon its optimistic press announcements. The court dismissed the suit, reasoning as follows:

> We doubt that nonspecific representations that an auction process is going well or going smoothly could in the circumstances of this case (the significance of this qualification will become clear shortly), influence a reasonable investor to pay more for a stock than he otherwise would. *Everybody* knows that someone trying to sell something is going to look and talk on the bright

1

■| Page 89.   2. Inquiries into the Materiality of Information |■

side. You don't sell a product by bad mouthing it. And everybody knows that auctions can be disappointing. It would be unreasonable for investors to attach significance to *general* expressions of satisfaction with the progress of the seller's efforts to sell, just as it would be unreasonable for them to infer from a potential bidder's apparent lack of enthusiasm that the bidder was uninterested rather than just was jockeying for a better price. The heart of a reasonable investor does not begin to flutter when a firm announces that some project or process is proceeding smoothly, and so the announcement will not drive up the price of the firm's shares to an unsustainable level.

... Suppose that on February 18 Centel's lawyers had told Centel that it couldn't legally sell any of its assets because they were encumbered and the lienors would not give their consent to a sale. In these circumstances to have announced that the auction process was going smoothly would have been materially deceptive. "Going smoothly" may mean nothing more than - going; but it means at least that; if the process had been stopped, a representation that it is continuing may well induce purchasers of the stock at a price that reflects the prospect that the process will continue to its end.

. . .

Centel was not, by its talk of smooth sailing, covering up a disaster. . . . The auction process was not interrupted. The results were disappointing, but that is a frequent outcome of auctions. . . .

An utterly candid statement of the company's hopes and fears, with emphasis on the fears, might well have pushed the company's stock below $40, but perhaps only because, given the expectation of puffing, such a statement would be taken to indicate that the prospects for the auction were much grimmer than they were. Where puffing is the order of the day, literal truth can be profoundly misleading, as senders and recipients of letters of recommendation well know. Mere sales puffery is not actionable under Rule 10b-5. . . .

Id. at 745-746 (emphasis original).

On the general topic of puffery under the securities laws, *see* Note, Securities Fraud or Mere Puffery: Refinement of the Corporate Puffery Defense, 51 Vand. L. Rev. 1049 (1998).

D. *Forward-Looking Information*

3. Management Discussion and Analysis

Page 89. Just before the heading, insert the following:

With the countdown toward the millennium much uncertainty lurks regarding the financial implications of the Year 2000 computer problem

2. Inquiries into the Materiality of Information

for SEC registrants. In Securities Act Release No. 7558 (July 29, 1998) the SEC provides specific guidance for registrants with respect to their disclosure obligations under various SEC rules and regulations, and most particularly with respect to the treatment of material events, trends, and uncertainties in management discussion and analysis portion of their SEC filings.

The release states that a company must provide Year 2000 disclosures if:

i) its assessment of its Year 2000 issues is not complete; or
ii) management determines that the consequences of its Year 2000 issues would have a material effect on the company's business, results or operations or financial condition, without taking into account the company's efforts to avoid those consequences.

Under the first test, the company should consider whether third parties, such as its suppliers and customers, are themselves Year 2000 compliant. This is material if their failure to be compliant will have a material effect on the registrant's business, results of operations, or financial condition. The SEC maintains that a registrant's assessment is not complete until it not only considers such third party effects but also takes reasonable steps to verify the Year 2000 readiness of any third party that could cause a material impact on the company.

Under the second test, in the absence of clear evidence of readiness, the registrant must evaluate whether it has a Year 2000 disclosure obligation assuming it will not be Year 2000 compliant. The resulting materiality determination is made on a "gross" basis. Under this test, the registrant is to assume that third parties that have not delivered written assurances of their own compliance will not be Year 2000 compliant. Significantly, the second test turns on estimates of the consequences if the company is not prepared, not on estimates of the cost to the company to become Year 2000 compliant.

Once the company determines it has a Year 2000 disclosure obligation it must decide what it should disclose. Here the release provides guidance by identifying the following four categories of information registrants must address:

1. state of readiness
2. cost to address Year 2000 issues
3. risks of Year 2000 issues
4. contingency plans

The release also reminds registrants that addressing the four categories above may not be sufficient to fulfill the company's disclosure obligations. The release, therefore, offers several other types of disclosures registrants may find necessary to include in their treatment of Year 2000 disclosures.

3

3

The Definition of a Security

H. Partnership Interests as Securities

Page 179. Insert the following case immediately preceding "Notes and Questions."

Steinhardt Group, Inc. v. Citicorp
126 F.3d 144 (10th Cir. 1997)

MANSMANN, J. In this appeal, we are asked to decide whether a highly structured securitization transaction negotiated between Citicorp and an investor in a limited partnership constitutes an "investment contract" as that term is defined by the Supreme Court in *SEC v. W.J. Howey Co.* Examining the economic reality of the transaction as a whole, we conclude that the limited partner retained pervasive control over its investment in the limited partnership such that it cannot be deemed a passive investor under *Howey* and its progeny. Accordingly, we find the securitization transaction here does not constitute an investment contract. . . .

I

The fraudulent conduct alleged in the amended complaint arises out of a severe financial crisis faced by Citicorp during the early 1990s. With bad loans and illiquid assets threatening the very existence of the nation's then-largest banking institution, Citicorp was looking for a way to extricate itself from its financial problems. The securitization transaction was thus conceived by Citicorp to remove the nonperforming assets from its financial books and replace them with cash.

In essence, the securitization required Citicorp to create an investment vehicle—a limited partnership ultimately named Bristol Oaks, L.P.—that would issue both debt securities, in the form of nonrecourse bonds, and equity securities, in the form of partnership interests, to investors. Bristol would acquire title to the nonperforming Mortgage Loans and REO [foreclosed] properties and would retain Ontra, Inc. to manage and liquidate the assets. Then Bristol would obtain bridge financing from Citibank . . . ; shortly thereafter, CSI [Citicorp Securities, Inc.] would securitize and underwrite a public offering of bonds and other debt securities to pay off the bridge financing. All of the investors' money was to be paid to Bristol and become the capital of that investment vehicle. The return on these investments was to come from the same pool of assets.

During late 1993 and the first half of 1994, representatives of CSI made a series of written and oral presentations to the Steinhardt Group in which they described returns of 18 percent or more annually by investing in Bristol. Throughout these presentations and in other meetings and telephone discussions, Citicorp explained how it had created the proprietary "Citicorp Non-Performing Loan Model" (the "Pricing Model"), based on its own past experience, intimate knowledge of the assets at issue, and the valuation of such assets. Citicorp represented the Pricing Model to be an accurate means of pricing the Mortgage Loans and REO properties in the portfolio and of providing the Steinhardt Group with the promised 18 percent or greater returns. In particular, Citicorp represented to the Steinhardt Group that no institution in America had more experience in single-family residential mortgages, or more knowledge about the process of collecting on defaulted mortgage loans. Moreover, Citicorp touted not only its longstanding reputation in the banking industry, but also how the assumptions in the Pricing Model were firmly grounded upon Citicorp's own unparalleled experience and expertise. . . .

According to the amended complaint, Citicorp knew at the time it made these representations that several of the assumptions underlying the Pricing Model were false. Steinhardt claims that Citicorp obtained inflated valuations by promising the brokers they would later be hired to list the properties for sale if the BPOs [Broker's Price Opinions] were satisfactory to Citicorp. The inflated valuations, in turn, caused the assets to be overpriced, which resulted in the overstatement of future cash flow. Steinhardt further contends that [Citicorp] failed to follow its own internal controls for insuring unbiased appraisals, that it employed brokers not on Citicorp's approved list, and that it required brokers to provide large numbers of valuations within grossly inadequate periods of time, which further undermined their accuracy. Although Citicorp was allegedly warned repeatedly by one of its own officers that the assets were overpriced, these warnings were never revealed to Steinhardt. Rather, Steinhardt contends these warnings were actively concealed in order to induce it to invest in Bristol.

According to the amended complaint, Citicorp concealed other information from Steinhardt, including the true cost of repairs and maintenance, low-end BPOs and other appraisals, recent appraisals which reflected the decline in the real estate market, the true cost and time for foreclosures, the true likelihood of delays caused by bankruptcy proceedings, and Citicorp's intention not to provide a conduit for the sale of reinstated loans. Steinhardt claims that "the cumulative effect of all these misrepresentations by Citicorp was to fraudulently inflate the purchase price for the entire portfolio."

Based on Citicorp's representations, Steinhardt entered into a letter agreement dated May 26, 1994 . . . in which it committed to make an equity contribution of between $40 million and $45 million in Bristol. According to the Letter Agreement, a portfolio of approximately $540 million to $660 million in Mortgage Loans and REO properties was to be sold by Citibank . . . to a newly formed limited partnership, Bristol. To fund the acquisition of the properties, Citibank . . . agreed to lend the newly formed partnership no less than 90 percent of the total purchase price; the remaining 10 percent was to be provided by the Partnership in the form of a cash payment representing the Partnership's total equity. Subsequently, debt securities were to be issued by the Partnership and underwritten by CSI to repay the Citibank . . . and CNAI loans.

The Letter Agreement further provided that "the Partnership will contract with Ontra, Inc. . . . , an independent third party who is experienced in loan servicing, loan workouts, REO sales, and oversight of these asset types," to service the properties. An affiliate of Ontra, BGO, was named the general partner of the new limited partnership in exchange for a 1 percent equity contribution. . . .

Steinhardt contends, Citibank's misrepresentation caused the assets to be overvalued by at least 25 percent. . . .

II

The outcome of this dispute hinges upon whether, under the circumstances, the securitization transaction constitutes an investment contract within the meaning of section 2(1) of the Securities Act of 1933. In order to invoke the protections of the federal securities laws, an investor must show, as a threshold matter, that the instrument in question is a security. Section 2(1) of the Act sets forth the definition of the term "security." Included in this definition are several catch-all categories which were designed to cover other securities interests not specifically enumerated in the statute. *See* Maura K. Monaghan, An Uncommon State of Confusion: The

Common Enterprise Element of Investment Contract Analysis, 63 Fordham L. Rev. 2135, 2136 (May 1995). One such category is the "investment contract." . . .

[Under *Howey*], the three requirements for establishing an investment contract are: (1) "an investment of money," (2) "in a common enterprise," (3) "with profits to come solely from the efforts of others." . . .

Clearly Steinhardt has alleged sufficient facts to meet the first prong of *Howey*. The Steinhardt Group, through its affiliate, C.B. Mtge., has invested $42 million in Bristol with the expectation of receiving a return on its investment of approximately 18 percent. . . .

Regarding the second prong, commonality, we have previously applied a horizontal commonality approach in determining whether a particular investment constitutes a security. *See Salcer v. Merrill Lynch, Pierce, Fenner and Smith*, 682 F.2d 459, 460 (3d Cir. 1982). "Horizontal commonality requires a pooling of investors' contributions and distribution of profits and losses on a pro-rata basis among investors." Monaghan, supra, at 2152-53. . . . Steinhardt argues that vertical commonality exists here and urges us to find that vertical commonality can satisfy the Howey common enterprise prong. . . . The Citicorp Defendants entreat us to find that Steinhardt negotiated such pervasive control over its investment in Bristol Oaks that it cannot meet the third element of *Howey*. . . .

. . . We do not need to consider whether vertical commonality should be adopted here, or whether horizontal community was adequately pleaded, because we believe the third element of *Howey* is dispositive.

The third prong of the Supreme Court's test in *Howey* requires that the purchaser be attracted to the investment by the prospect of a profit on the investment rather than a desire to use or consume the item purchased. *United Housing Foundation, Inc. v. Forman*, 421 U.S. 837, 853-54 (1975) (court concluded that sale of shares in a housing cooperative did not give rise to a securities transaction where none of the promotional materials emphasized profit and there was a low probability the shares would actually produce a profit). In analyzing this element, the courts have also looked at whether the investor has meaningfully participated in the management of the partnership in which it has invested such that it has more than minimal control over the investment's performance. Monaghan, supra, at 2151. . . .

To resolve the issue of whether Steinhardt's involvement in the Bristol Oaks Limited Partnership was limited to that of a passive investor, we must look at the transaction as a whole, considering the arrangements the parties made for the operation of the investment vehicle in order to determine who exercised control in generating profits for the vehicle. The Limited Partnership Agreement ("LPA"), which establishes the relative powers of the partners in running the enterprise, therefore governs our inquiry.

Section 3.1(f) of the LPA, as amended, requires that "the Managing

Partner shall not have the right to take any of the following actions ("Material Actions") without the consent of ... a Majority of the Partners (or pursuant to an approved Business Plan).... " The "Material Actions," set forth in section 3.1(f) of the LPA, include most tasks that are crucial to turning the mortgages and REO into profit, which is the basic purpose of Bristol Oaks, *e.g.*, entering into any written or verbal material agreement or transaction with any borrower outside of the Loan Documents; giving any material consent required to be obtained by any borrower under the Loan Documents; modifying or amending any of the Loan Documents; exercising any rights under the Loan Documents; selling, exchanging, securitizing, conveying, or otherwise voluntarily disposing of, or placing any encumbrance on, the Properties. Under the LPA, a "Majority of the Partners" is defined as "those Partners holding greater than fifty percent (50 percent) of the Percentage Interests...", meaning that Steinhardt alone constitutes a "Majority of the Partners."

Steinhardt approved the interim business plan and, although Citicorp drafted that plan, Steinhardt retains the power to amend that plan as it wishes in one of two ways: (1) in its capacity as "Majority of the Partners," Steinhardt can propose and approve a new business plan; or (2) if the general partner proposes a new business plan, Steinhardt retains veto power, which it can exercise merely by declining to approve the proposed change within fifteen business days. Thus, we agree with the Citicorp Defendants that "Steinhardt's consent is required for the taking of any 'Material Action,' whether through its control over the business plan, or through its veto power over 'Material Actions' that fall outside the parameters of the business plan."

The LPA further provides that where a Majority of the Partners proposes a Material Action, the general partner "shall use best efforts to implement such Material Action at the Partnership's expense on the terms proposed by such Majority of the Partners," *i.e.*, Steinhardt. If the general partner refuses to act with such best efforts in pursuit of Steinhardt's proposals, Steinhardt can remove and replace the general partner without notice.

As the above provisions demonstrate, the LPA gives Steinhardt pervasive control over the management of the Partnership. Indeed, these quite significant powers are far afield of the typical limited partnership agreement whereby a limited partner leaves the control of the business to the general partners. We find the agreement altogether consistent with the arrangement before us: Steinhardt, a sophisticated investor, made a $42 million capital contribution in Bristol Oaks, thereby becoming a 98.79 percent partner through a highly negotiated transaction.

Moreover, it appears the parties have carefully constructed the LPA to give Steinhardt significant control without possibly running afoul of the Delaware Revised Uniform Limited Partnership Act, 6 Del. C. § 17-101, et seq. Indeed, Steinhardt has proposal and approval rights rather than more affirmative responsibilities. We also find unpersuasive Steinhardt's contention that its powers were limited under the LPA. First, Steinhardt points out language in the LPA that:

> except for specific rights to propose and approve or disapprove certain Partnership matters as set forth in the Agreement, the Limited Partners shall not take any part whatsoever in, or have any control over, the business or affairs of the Partnership, nor shall the Limited Partners have any right or authority to act for or bind the Partnership.

Given the extensive proposal and approval rights retained by Steinhardt under the LPA, the "except" clause swallows the general rule of nonparticipation. Second, Steinhardt points out that if a business plan was in place, as it was as soon as Steinhardt approved the interim agreement, Steinhardt's approval was not required for the general partner to take Material Actions. Steinhardt's argument lacks substance, however, since Steinhardt could amend the business plan at any time, and the general partner needed Steinhardt's approval to take any Material Action not provided for under the business plan.

At oral argument, counsel for Steinhardt made a corollary argument that since the interim agreement was in place, the general partner could operate the partnership without Steinhardt exercising the authority given to it under the LPA. . . . However, the issue does not turn on whether the investor actually exercised its rights, but rather, on what "legal rights and powers [were] enjoyed by the investor." Moreover, on a 12(b)(6) motion, we must consider the commercial realities of the transaction and, in doing so, we conclude that without Steinhardt's involvement, the Partnership could only operate in a static, inflexible way that is unrealistic and impractical in today's business climate.

Steinhardt further argues that the Delaware Revised Uniform Limited Partnership Act supports its position that it was a passive investor. The Act enumerates those actions of the limited partners that do not equate to controlling the management of the partnership and includes many of the approval rights given to Steinhardt. Steinhardt submits that since under the Act it would not be deemed to have exercised control, it must be a passive investor for *Howey* purposes.

We find that the Act is not controlling here. The LPA states "except as otherwise expressly provided in this Agreement, the rights and duties of the Partners and the administration and termination of the Partnership shall be governed by the Act." The Act defines control, however, solely for the purpose of limiting the liability of the limited partners to third parties— a situation not present here. 6 Del. C. § 17-303(b). This does not necessarily equate to the threshold for finding a passive investor under federal securities laws. The Delaware Act puts third parties on notice that just because limited partners undertake certain responsibilities with regard to the management of the partnership, that does not make them liable for the obligations of the partnership. Here, Steinhardt is not trying to shield itself from liability, but rather, is seeking relief for alleged violations of federal securities laws. Federal law therefore determines whether the investor's involvement is significant enough to place it outside the role of a passive investor.

Thus, accepting, as we must, the facts as alleged in the amended complaint, we do not find Steinhardt is entitled to relief under *Howey* and its progeny.

III

We find that the rights and powers assigned to Steinhardt under the LPA were not nominal, but rather, were significant and, thus, directly affected the profits it received from the Partnership. Accordingly, we hold Steinhardt's investment in the Bristol Oaks Limited Partnership does not constitute an investment contract. . . .

4
The Public Offering

B. Registration Under the '33 Act

4. Preparation and Review of the Registration Statement

Page 268. Add the following subsection immediately before section 5, *Shelf Registrations Under Rule 415.*

c. Plain English Disclosures

The SEC adopted Rule 421(b) and (d) to require registrants to use "plain English" in writing certain portions of the registration statement and accompanying prospectus. Securities Act Release No. 7497 (Jan. 28, 1998). The purpose is to make the prospectus clear, concise, and easy-to-read rather than filled with dense, turgid, and hard-to-read legalese. The SEC proposal specifies six minimum plain English principles that registrants will be required to use in drafting the front and back cover pages as well as the "summary" and "risk factors" sections of the prospectus:

- active voice
- short sentences
- everyday language
- tabular presentation of complex material
- no legal jargon, and
- no multiple negatives

The overall objective of the proposal is to make the prospectus a less forbidding document so that investors will have an interest in examining its many parts. To accomplish this objective, the SEC proposes not only to make the front and back pages more readable but also to amend its rules so that certain technical information (for example, information regarding the underwriters' stabilization activities or the availability of the issuer's Exchange Act reports) now required to appear on the front and back pages of the prospectus will be disclosed in the body of the prospectus. The SEC encourages issuers to use its proposed plain English requirements in drafting all disclosure documents.

The following are some of the SEC's illustrations of how plain English can make the prospectus more readable:

Before / After

Active Voice

Before	After
No person has been authorized to give any information or make any representation other than those contained or incorporated by reference in this joint proxy statement/prospectus, and, if given or made, such information or representation must not be relied upon as having been authorized.	You should rely only on the information contained in this document or incorporated by reference. We have not authorized anyone to provide you with information that is different.

Short Sentences

Before	After
Machine Industries and Great Tools, Inc., are each subject to the information requirements of the Securities Exchange Act of 1934, as amended (the "Exchange Act"), and in accordance therewith file reports, proxy statements, and other information with the Securities and Exchange Commission (the "Commission").	We must comply with the Securities Exchange Act of 1934. Accordingly, we file annual, quarterly and current reports, proxy statements, and other information with the Securities and Exchange Commission.

Definite, Concrete, Everyday Language

Before	After
History of Net Losses. The Company has reorded a net loss under generally accepted accounting principles for each fiscal year since its inception in May 1990, as well as for the nine months ended June 30, 1995. However, these results include the effect of certain significant, non-cash accounting charges related to the accounting for the Company's acquisitions and related transactions.	**History of Net Losses.** We have recorded a net loss under generally accepted accounting principles for each year since we started in 1990, and for the nine months ended June 30, 1995. Our losses were caused, in part, by the annual write-off of a portion of the goodwill resulting from the ten acquisitions we made during this period.

No Legal Jargon or Highly Technical Business Terms

Before	After
The new debt will rank *pari passu* with other senior debt of the company.	The new debt will rank equally with the other senior debt of the company.

■| 4. The Public Offering

The following description encompasses all the material terms and provisions of the Notes offered hereby and supplements, and to the extent inconsistent therewith replaces, the description of the general terms and provisions of the Debt Securities (as defined in the accompanying Prospectus) set forth under the heading "Description of Debt Securities" in the Prospectus, to which description reference is hereby made.	We disclose information about our notes in two separate documents that progressively provide more detail on the note's specific terms: the prospectus, and this pricing supplement. Since the specific terms of notes are made at the time of pricing, rely on information in the pricing supplement over different information in the prospectus.

No Multiple Negatives

No clause can become valid unless approved by both parties.	A clause becomes valid only if both parties approve it.

Before issuing its present proposals, the SEC in the spring of 1996 commenced a pilot program of encouraging companies to draft their registration statements and other SEC disclosures in plain English. As an incentive for companies to dabble with plain English, the SEC offered expedited review of their documents. Exhibits 4-1 and 4-2 illustrate the effects of not only plain English but the SEC permitting some information to be relocated to other portion's of the prospectus.

Writing in plain English, of course, may well be just a matter of perspective. On this point, consider the annual reports of Berkshire Hathaway, Inc., which have long been admired for the clear and folksy prose of their author, Berkshire's chairman and legendary investor Warren Buffett. Consider Buffet's description of Berkshire's insurance operations, one of the company's many activities:

> [W]e sell policies that insurance and reinsurance companies buy to protect themselves from the effects of mega-catastrophes. Since truly major catastrophes are rare occurrences, our super-cat business can be expected to show large profits in most years—and to record a huge loss occasionally. In other words, the attractiveness of our super-cat business will take a great many years to measure. *What you must understand, however, is that a truly terrible year in the super-cat business is not a possibility—it's a certainty. The only question is when it will come.*
>
> I emphasize this lugubrious point because I would not want you to panic and sell your Berkshire stock upon hearing that some large catastrophe had cost us a significant amount. If you would tend to react that way, you should not own Berkshire shares now, just as you should entirely avoid owning stocks if a crashing market would lead you to panic and sell. Selling fine businesses on "scary" news is usually a bad decision. . . .

15

EXHIBIT 4-1

$225,000,000

Baltimore Gas and Electric Company
Medium-Term Notes, Series D
Due from 9 months to 30 years from Date of Issue

BEFORE

Baltimore Gas and Electric Company (the "Company") intends to sell from time to time up to $225,000,000 aggregate principal amount of its unsecured Medium-Term Notes, Series D (the "Notes"). Each Note will mature from 9 months to 30 years from the date of issue as determined by mutual agreement of the initial purchasers and the Company. The Notes may be subject to optional redemption prior to their stated maturity as indicated in an accompanying supplement to this Prospectus (the "Pricing Supplement") but will not be subject to conversion, amortization or any sinking fund.

The interest rate, or interest rate formula, for each Note will be established by the Company at the date of issuance of such Note and will be indicated in the applicable Pricing Supplement. Each interest-bearing Note will bear interest at either (a) a fixed rate (a "Fixed Rate Note") or (b) a variable rate determined by reference to an interest rate formula (a "Floating Rate Note"), which may be adjusted by adding or subtracting a Spread or multiplying by a Spread Multiplier, as indicated in the applicable Pricing Supplement. Unless otherwise indicated in the applicable Pricing Supplement, the interest rate formula for Floating Rate Notes will be the Commercial Paper Rate, the Prime Rate, the CD Rate, the Federal Funds Effective Rate, LIBOR, the Treasury Rate, or the CMT Rate. Interest rates, or interest rate formulas, are subject to change by the Company from time to time, but no such change will affect any Note previously issued or which the Company has agreed to sell. Unless otherwise indicated in the applicable Pricing Supplement, the interest payment dates for Fixed Rate Notes will be each May 1 and November 1; the interest payment dates for Floating Rate Notes will be specified in the applicable Pricing Supplement. See "DESCRIPTION OF NOTES."

The Notes will be issued in minimum denominations of $100,000 and integral multiples of $1,000 in excess thereof. Notes may be issued, as specified in the applicable Pricing Supplement, in definitive form or may be represented by a permanent global Note or Notes registered in the name of The Depository Trust Company, as depositary (the "Depositary"), or a nominee of the Depositary (each such Note represented by a permanent global Note being referred to herein as a "Book-Entry Note"). Beneficial interests in Book-Entry Notes will only be evidenced by, and transfers thereof will only be effected through, records maintained by the Depositary (with respect to its participants) and the Depositary's participants (with respect to beneficial owners). Except as described under "DESCRIPTION OF NOTES—Book-Entry Notes," owners of beneficial interests in a permanent global Note will not be entitled to receive physical delivery of Notes in definitive form and will not be considered the holders thereof.

THESE SECURITIES HAVE NOT BEEN APPROVED OR DISAPPROVED BY THE SECURITIES AND EXCHANGE COMMISSION OR ANY STATE SECURITIES COMMISSION NOR HAS THE SECURITIES AND EXCHANGE COMMISSION OR ANY STATE SECURITIES COMMISSION PASSED UPON THE ACCURACY OR ADEQUACY OF THIS PROSPECTUS. ANY REPRESENTATION TO THE CONTRARY IS A CRIMINAL OFFENSE.

	Price to Public (1)	Agents' Commission (2)(3)	Proceeds to Company (2)(4)
Per Note	100%	.125% - .750%	99.875% - 99.250%
Total	$225,000,000	$281,250 - $1,687,500	$224,718,750 - $223,312,500

(1) Unless otherwise indicated in a Pricing Supplement, Notes will be issued at 100% of their principal amount.
(2) The Company will pay Lehman Brothers, Lehman Brothers Inc., and Goldman, Sachs & Co. (the "Agents"), as agents, a commission ranging from .125% to .750% of the principal amount of any Note, depending on its stated maturity, sold through any such Agent. The Company also may sell Notes to any Agent at a discount for resale to one or more purchasers at varying prices related to prevailing market prices at the time of resale, as determined by such Agent. In the case of Notes sold directly to investors by the Company, no discount will be allowed or commission paid.
(3) The Company has agreed to indemnify the Agents against certain civil liabilities under the Securities Act of 1933.
(4) Before deduction of expenses payable by the Company estimated at $330,000.

The Notes will be offered on a continuing basis by the Company through the Agents, each of which has agreed to use all reasonable efforts to solicit purchases of the Notes. The Company reserves the right to sell Notes directly to purchasers on its own behalf. The Company also may sell Notes to either Agent acting as principal for resale to one or more purchasers. The Company reserves the right to withdraw, cancel or modify the offer made hereby without notice. The Company or any Agent may reject any offer to purchase Notes, in whole or in part. See "PLAN OF DISTRIBUTION OF NOTES."

LEHMAN BROTHERS   **GOLDMAN, SACHS & CO.**

September 8, 1995

■| 4. The Public Offering

EXHIBIT 4-2

PROSPECTUS

**$200,000,000
MEDIUM-TERM NOTES
SERIES E**

AFTER

BGE

Baltimore Gas and Electric Company
39 W. Lexington Street
Baltimore, Maryland 21201
(410) 234-5000

TERMS OF SALE

The following terms may apply to the notes which we may sell at one or more times. The final terms for each note will be included in a pricing supplement. For more detail, see "Description of Notes." We will receive between $199,750,000 and $198,500,000 of the proceeds from the sale of the notes, after paying the agents commissions of between $250,000 and $1,500,000.

- Mature 9 months to 30 years
- Fixed or floating interest rate. The floating interest rate formula would be based on:
    ◊ Commercial paper rate
    ◊ Prime rate
    ◊ CD rate
    ◊ Federal Funds effective rate
    ◊ LIBOR
    ◊ Treasury rate
    ◊ CMT rate

- Remarketing features
- Certificate or book-entry form
- Subject to redemption and repurchase at option of BGE or holder
- Not convertible, amortized or subject to a sinking fund
- Interest paid on fixed rate notes on May 1 and November 1
- Interest paid on floating rate notes monthly, quarterly, semi-annually, or annually
- Minimum denominations of $1,000, increased in multiples of $1,000

The notes have not been approved by the SEC or any state securities commission, nor have these organizations determined that this prospectus is accurate or complete. Any representation to the contrary is a criminal offense.

LEHMAN BROTHERS   GOLDMAN, SACHS & CO.
AGENTS

January 6, 1997

1996 Annual Report, Berkshire Hathaway, Inc. at 8 (italics original). Incidentally, Mr. Buffett reveals that his own preparation for using plain English is that he pretends he is talking to his sisters. He suggests that SEC registrants begin their reports with "Dear Doris and Bertie:"

Many securities lawyers have openly expressed their concern that compliance with the SEC's plain English rules could prevent issuers from expressing complex concepts in their prospectus and thereby increase their liability under the securities laws. Do you agree? Is the proposal consistent with how informationally efficient markets function? Is the proposal better directed toward issuers qualified to use Form S-3 or those that cannot take advantage of the SEC's integrated disclosure procedures?

C. Gun Jumping

2. The Waiting Period

c. Selling Practices During the Waiting Period

Page 298. Add the following new material before the Problems.

Road shows, which take place after the registration statement is filed and before it is declared effective, are used to create and assess interest in the offering. The typical road show is attended by, on the one hand, underwriters and officers of the issuer, and, on the other hand, analysts, securities professionals, and institutional investors. Retail customers are excluded. Because presentations are oral and the only distributed written document is a preliminary prospectus, road shows do not run afoul of Section 5(b)(1). In a series of no-action letters, the SEC approves the increasing use of electronic media for road shows. In Net Roadshow, Inc. SEC No-Action Letter (Sept. 8, 1997), the agency approved an arrangement whereby prequalified individuals of the type customarily invited to live road shows would be granted a password to access the underwriter's website where it could view a film of the entire live road show; viewers could download the preliminary prospectus but not the road show presentation. Further broadening the use of electronic media for road shows is Private Financial Network (PFN), SEC No-Action Letter (March 12, 1997), where the staff concurred in the reasoning that "radio" and "television," as used in Section 2(10), apply only to such communications when they are "widely disseminated to an undifferentiated public." The staff thus believed that PFN's proposal to transmit road shows via video teleconferencing and closed-circuit television to an audience prescreened by PFN would not

■| 4. The Public Offering   Page 308. |■

violate Section 5. It should be noted here that PFN stated it would provide its subscribers with a copy of the preliminary prospectus and would require subscribers to agree not to copy or further distribute the road show transmission.

Page 308.   Insert the following at the end of the second full paragraph and before the heading.

4.   Reforming the Public Offering Process—The "Aircraft Carrier" Release

The SEC has proposed extensive changes for the regulation of securities offerings. Securities Act Release No. 7606 (November 3, 1998). The sweeping proposals are set forth in a release that is commonly referred to as the "aircraft carrier" release, an expression that aptly captures the breadth of its numerous proposals as well as the fact that they are embodied in a 584-page release. In broad overview, the SEC proposes to replace existing registration forms with two main forms—Form B and Form A. Form B would be an abbreviated registration form similar to current Form S-3 (or its counterpart for foreign issuers, F-3), and Form A would replace Forms S-1 and S-2 (and Forms F-1 and F-2 for foreign issuers). A third form, Form C, would be available for business combinations. All the proposed forms would be used by domestic and foreign issuers alike.

Under the aircraft carrier proposal, Form B's basic eligibility requirement is that the issuer must have at least a public equity float of $75 million (the same as now currently required for Form S-3) and must also have an average daily trading volume of $1 million (an issuer with a public float of at least $250 million is eligible regardless of its average daily trading volume). The proposal provides several alternative bases for an issuer's offer to occur on Form B. One such alternative basis is for seasoned issuers who propose to make an offering only to qualified institutional buyers (institutional investors of the type discussed later in Chapter 6 who own a portfolio of at least $100 million). Another alternative eligibility requirement applies to a seasoned issuer's offering of nonconvertible investment grade securities. Seasoned issuer for Form B is defined to include issuers who have been a reporting company for one year, are current in their Exchange Act reporting requirements, and have not during that year failed to meet a dividend, interest, or lease obligation. Issuers that are not eligible for Form B must register their public offerings on Form A. Offerings on Form B would incorporate much of the registration statement information from the issuer's Exchange Act reports that would be supplemented by updating that information through a "securities term sheet," as well as "offering information" that relates to information describing the offering transaction. Issuers that have been a reporting company for 24 months but fail to meet Form B's public float requirement may also incorporate on Form A information from the Exchange Act reports, provided they have filed at least two annual reports with the SEC. The following lists some of the important regulatory changes proposed in the aircraft carrier release.

Free Writing. Recall that currently sales materials and other communications that are not a formal part of the registration statement cannot be used until the registration statement becomes effective. The proposal relaxes this prohibition so that all issuers may engage in extensive free writing before the registration statement becomes effective.

Delayed and Continuous Offerings. As proposed, Form B issuers are not required to file a registration statement until the first *sale* of securities. Before filing, Form B issuers and their underwriters may, therefore, engage in selling efforts, including the distribution of written offering materials. The SEC will not conduct a formal review of the filed Form B; it will merely screen the registration statement to ensure the issuers are eligible to use Form B. If this portion of the proposal is adopted, does it obviate the need for the shelf registration provision currently embodied in Rule 415(a)(1)(x)? On the topic of delayed offerings, the SEC's proposals are less radical for Form A qualified issuers who must file their registration statement before making any offer. However, certain medium-sized and small *seasoned* issuers, though not eligible to use Form B, will have the flexibility to control the timing of their offering by being able to identify the time and date that their registration statement will become effective. For these issuers, the SEC will not conduct a formal review of the registration statement. Thus, staff review and the resulting comfort letter will occur only for nonseasoned issuers. Overall, the SEC hopes its proposals introduce significant flexibility so that issuers will be encouraged to register an increased number of offerings rather than raise capital through exemptions, a topic discussed in the next chapter.

Communications During Prefiling Period. The aircraft carrier release proposes a radical departure from existing restrictions on communications during the offering process. The SEC proposes that Form B registrants remove all existing restrictions on communications during the prefiling period. As for Form A registrants, the SEC proposes a safe harbor for all communications made more than 30 days before the filing date of the registration statement.

Research Reports. The proposal would significantly revise Rule 139, the primary rule governing the publication of research reports by broker-dealers. No restriction would apply for research reports regarding Form B offerings or for reports regarding Form A issuers that occur more than 30 days before the filing date of the registration statement. Even within this 30-day period, the SEC proposes to permit so-called "focus reports," which are research reports on seasoned domestic issuers or large foreign issuers.

Prospectus Delivery Requirements. Throughout the aircraft carrier releases the emphasis is on maximizing the information that is made available to investors and making the information available to them on a timely basis. This is best illustrated by the proposals dealing with the delivery of a prospectus. Here the importance of the final prospectus is deemphasized by refocusing regulatory efforts on the dissemination of information before the investors make their decision to purchase.

The proposals call for the repeal of Rule 434 and the substituting of a requirement that investors receive a preliminary prospectus and be advised, prior to the delivery of a confirmation of sale, where they can obtain a final prospectus (for example, from the issuer's Web site). The latter procedure will also fulfill the dealer's after-market prospectus delivery obligation. For Form A issuers, the proposal calls for *delivery* of the prospectus at least seven calendar-days before the date the offering is priced (this time period is shortened to three days for seasoned issuers). In the case of Form B registrants, the SEC is seeking comment on two alternative approaches, each of which requires *delivery* of certain transaction-specific information to the investors prior to pricing the offering.

Small Business Issuers. The release proposes to raise the annual revenue ceiling for issuers qualified to use the small business issuer registration procedures from $25 million to $50 million and to remove the public float limitation.

Periodic Reporting Enhancements. The SEC is proposing to shorten the time period within which issuers must file their annual and quarterly reports to greater enhance risk factor disclosures in their Exchange Act reports and to expand the range of events that will trigger the requirement to file Form 8-K.

Underwriter Due Diligence Investigations. A recurrent concern among underwriters is their due diligence obligations under section 11 of the Securities Act. Section 11 imposes liability on underwriters (and selected others) for any material omission or misstatement in the registration statement unless they prove that after reasonable investigation the underwriter had a reasonable basis to believe, and did believe, the registration statement did not contain any material misrepresentation when it became effective. The underwriters' concern is exacerbated by any regulatory development that quickens the process by which issuers are able to run the regulatory gauntlet on their way to the market; any shortening of the regulatory period reduces the time that underwriters have to carry out their due diligence investigation. The aircraft carrier release proposes to broaden the existing due diligence safe harbor Rule 176 to include a general reference to six practices that courts should view positively when evaluating the underwriter's due diligence defense. The SEC also invites comment on the possibility that underwriters could meet their due diligence obligation by relying on a report of a "qualified independent professional" who has reviewed the registrant's Exchange Act reports that will be incorporated by reference into its registration statement.

The aircraft carrier release portends the most fundamental change to the operation of the Securities Act since integrated disclosure was introduced in 1982. The release, however, has met with a decided coolness on the part of the financial community, which faults it for not going further in liberating clients from regulations that are seen as being profoundly out of touch with today's marketplace. It will, therefore, be interesting to see whether the aircraft carrier will return to the dock to be refitted as "aircraft carrier II."

F. *The International Public Offering*

2. Offerings Outside the United States: Regulation S

Page 332. Add the following update before the Notes and Questions.

Update: In 1998, the SEC amended Regulation S to address abuses of Regulation S by some U.S. issuers under the safe harbor's original provisions. Securities Act Release No. 7505 (February 17, 1998). As will be seen, the cumulative effect of the amendments is to restrict the freedom of *U.S.* issuers to raise capital outside the United States in reliance upon Regulation S. This occurs because the amendments impose on U.S. issuers that are reporting companies the same demanding limitations that previously applied only to nonreporting issuers when making an offering of their equity securities. No change was introduced by the amendments for foreign issuers or debt offerings by U.S. issuers.

The most significant amendment to Regulation S occurred in Rule 903(B)(3) which now requires that any equity security sold in reliance upon the safe harbor is subject to offering and resale restrictions for one year. Previously reporting companies selling securities were subject to a forty-day restricted period (now called the "distribution compliance period"). After the amendment, equity security offerings of *all* U.S. issuers made in reliance upon Regulation S cannot be resold in the United States for a one-year period absent registration or an exemption for such resale.

The amendment also requires that purchasers (other than distributors)

■I 4. The Public Offering Page 334. I■

of such equity securities of U.S. issuers must certify they are not U.S. persons and that they are not acquiring the securities for the benefit of a U.S. person. Purchasers must also agree to sell the equity security only in accordance with the registration or exemptive provisions of the Securities Act. The U.S. issuer of equity securities must have in place a stop transfer provision to prevent resales that are not in accordance with Regulation S. Also, the certificates for the shares must bear a restrictive legend that no resales should occur that are in violation of the Securities Act. Prior to its amendment, such certifications, agreements, transfer restrictions, and legends only applied to nonreporting U.S. issuers.

The SEC also adopted new Rule 905, which classifies equity securities sold in reliance upon Regulation S as "restricted securities." The full understanding of this designation is examined in Chapter 6. Such designation effectively means that a Regulation S equity security cannot be resold in the United States without registration or an applicable exemption for such resale. Though Regulation S provides a one-year compliance period during which no resales of any kind may occur in the United States, this does not mean that at the end of one year the securities can be freely resold in the United States. Indeed, as a consequence of the Regulation S shares now being restricted securities, it means that limitations on their resale will likely be longer than the one-year compliance period now imposed by Regulation S. This occurs because under the standard resale safe harbor of Rule 144 limitations on resale continues until two years have elapsed since the shares were first sold by the issuer. These requirements are examined more closely in Chapter 6.

Finally, U.S. issuers are now required to report Regulation S sales of equity securities on a quarterly basis on Form 10-Q.

Page 334. Add the following new material after the carryover paragraph and before the Problems.

4. Press Coverage for Foreign Issuers. Some foreign countries, unlike the U.S., permit companies offering securities for sale to conduct press conferences, issue press releases, and meet with members of the press during the offering. Though they have typically excluded U.S. journalists, the information ultimately was reported in the U.S. press, albeit usually later than in the foreign press. Because the SEC believed U.S. investors were placed at a competitive disadvantage by the exclusion of the U.S.-based journalists from such conferences, the SEC adopted Rule 135e. The rule provides it is not an offer to sell a security if a *foreign* issuer or its representatives permit journalists to attend press conferences or meetings with the issuer or its representatives where information related to a present or proposed public offering of securities will be released. The exemption

■I Page 334.　　　　　　　　　　　　　4. The Public Offering I■

is conditioned on the press conference being held outside the United States and that the security offering will not occur solely in the United States. Is Rule 135e fair to a U.S. issuer who contemplates selling its shares in the United States and England?

5. *Beyond Regulation S.* In *Europe and Overseas Commodity Traders, S.A. v. Banque Paribas London,* 147 F.3d 118 (2d Cir. 1998), the court found that Section 5 was not violated by a transaction that clearly fell outside Regulation S. Carr, the sole shareholder and agent of EOC, a Panamanian company with a mailing address in Monaco, commenced discussions in London with Arida, a U.K. national, regarding a substantial investment EOC could make through Arida. Carr then departed to Florida for some much needed rest, where he had further communications with Arida both by phone and fax. The court found that Carr approved the purchase by EOC of shares from Arida while he was in Florida. Carr, later believing that Arida had lied to him, sued under the Exchange Act's antifraud provision and for rescission under Section 12(a)(1), alleging Arida had sold a security in the U.S. in violation of Section 5.

The Second Circuit had no trouble concluding that no Regulation S safe harbor was available because of the communications that occurred while Carr was in Florida. However, the court reasoned that the conduct and effects test that has developed in connection with the antifraud provision's extraterritorial application can be adapted to a transaction that falls outside the Regulation S safe harbor.

> The conduct and effect test was developed by the courts in the absence of clear Congressional guidance as to the jurisdictional reach of the antifraud provisions of the securities laws. . . . The antifraud provisions are designed to remedy deceptive and manipulative conduct with the potential to harm the public interest or the interests of investors. . . . However, because it is well-settled in this Circuit that "anti-fraud provisions of American securities laws have broader extraterritorial reach than American filing requirements," [*Consolidated Gold Fields,* 871 F.2d] . . . at 262, the extent of conduct or effect in the United States needed to invoke U.S. jurisdiction over a claimed violation of the registration provisions must be greater than that which would trigger U.S. jurisdiction over a claim of fraud. To adapt the conduct and effects test for use in interpreting the registration provisions, we must take into account Congress' distinct purpose in drafting the registration laws. . . .
>
> Through mandatory disclosure, Congress sought to promote informed investing and to deter the kind of fraudulent salesmanship that was believed to have led to the market collapse of 1929. . . . The registration provisions are thus prophylactic in nature. Seen in this light, the registration provisions also can be said to aim at certain conduct with the potential for discernible effects. Specifically, the registration provisions are designed to prevent the offer of securities in the United States securities markets without accompany-

4. The Public Offering — Page 334.

ing standardized disclosures to aid investors, a course of conduct. The conduct, in turn, has the effect of creating interest in and demand for unregistered securities. To avoid this result ... the registration provisions should apply to those offers of unregistered securities that tend to have the effect of creating a market for unregistered securities in the United States; and by "creating a market" we do not mean that the conduct must be directed at a large number of people.

The Commission's release accompanying Regulation S ... support the application of this conduct and effects test.

The nearly de minimis U.S. interest in the transactions presented in the instant case precludes our finding that U.S. jurisdiction exists under the more limited conduct and effect standard appropriate under the registration provisions of the 1933 Act. Under the facts as alleged by EOC, there was conduct in the United States because Arida called Carr here and Carr executed his order here. However, the conduct was not such as to have the effect of creating a market for those securities in the United States. Carr's presence here was entirely fortuitous and personal and the actual purchaser of shares ... was an offshore corporation without a place of business here.

The court's opinion in dismissing the antifraud claim for want of subject matter jurisidiction appears in Supplement Chapter 18.

5
Exempt Transactions

D. Regulation D and the Limited Offering Exemptions

5. Limitations on the Manner and Scope of an Offering

Page 411. Insert the following update at the end of the section.

Update: In 1999, the Commission amended Rule 504 to address fraudulent practices associated with the marketing of "microcap" companies. It explained:

> In some cases, Rule 504 has been used in fraudulent schemes to make prearranged "sales" of securities under the rule to nominees in states that do not have registration or prospectus delivery requirements. As a part of this arrangement, these securities are then placed with broker-dealers who use cold-calling techniques to sell the securities at ever-increasing prices to unknowing investors. When their inventory of shares is exhausted, these firms permit the artificial market demand created to collapse, and investors lose much, if not all, of their investment. This scheme is sometimes colloquially referred to as "pump and dump."

Securities Act Release No. 7644 (Feb. 26, 1999).

As proposed, the amendments would have extended to Rule 504 the restrictions on resale applicable under Rules 505 and 506. Commenters objected to a blanket restriction because it would create a significant liquidity discount that would effectively reduce the capital that small issuers could raise under the exemption. As adopted, the amendments key general solicitation and restrictions on resale for Rule 504 offerings on the presence

▌▎ Pages 411–412. 　　　　　　　　**5. Exempt Transactions ▎▌**

of state regulation of the offerings. General solicitation and restricted securities limitations will apply unless the offering is (1) registered under state law requiring public filing and delivery of a disclosure document to investors before sale, or (2) exempted under state law that permits general solicitation and advertising as long as sales are made only to accredited investors as defined in Rule 501(a). In its adopting release, the Commission commented on the operative effective of the amendments: "Since most transactions under Rule 504 are private ones, they will continue to be permissible under the exemption, but general solicitation and advertising will not be permitted and the securities will be 'restricted.'"

6. Determining the Aggregate Offering Price in Offerings Under Rules 504 and 505

Pages 411–412. *Correction:* Delete the parenthetical statement (referencing a $500,000 limitation) in the carryover lines on these pages.

8. Additional Regulation D Requirements and Features

Page 417. Add the following update immediately prior to the question.

Update: Rule 504 was amended in 1999 to extend restrictions on resale to many (perhaps most) Rule 504 offerings. For further discussion, please see the above update insert for page 411 of the text.

E. *Employee Plans and Contracts Relating to Compensation: Rule 701*

Page 423. Add the following update immediately prior to the Notes and Questions.

Update: Commenting that "the $5 million [aggregate offering price] limit appears to have become unnecessarily restrictive in light of inflation, the increased popularity of equity ownership as a retention and incentive

5. Exempt Transactions

device for employees, and the growth of deferred compensation plans," the Commission in 1999 approved amendments to Rule 701 that:

(1) remove the $5 million aggregate offering price ceiling and, instead, set the maximum amount of securities *that may be sold* in a year at the greatest of:

—$1 million (rather than the current $500,000);
—15 percent of the issuer's total assets; or
—15 percent of the outstanding securities of that class;

(2) require the issuer to provide specific disclosure to each purchaser of securities *if* more than $5 million worth of securities are to be sold;
(3) do not count offers for purposes of calculating the available exempted amounts;
(4) harmonize the definition of consultants and advisors permitted to use the exemption to the narrower definition of Form S-8 (the short-form registration statement form for the offer and sale of employee benefit plan securities); and
(5) simplify the rule by recasting it in plain English.

Existing restrictions on resale of securities sold under Rule 701 are unaffected by the 1999 amendments.

6

Secondary Distributions

D. *Rule 144—Safe Harbor for Resales of Control and Restricted Securities*

Page 467. Add the following update to the first paragraph under "Holding Period."

Update: In 1997, the SEC amended Rule 144 to shorten the holding period from that described on page 467. As amended, Rule 144's safe harbor is not available for a restricted security unless one year has elapsed between the security's issuance and its resale. Restricted securities meeting this one-year requirement must also comply with the requirements in Rule 144(c), (e), (f), and (h) pertaining to there being certain public information about the issuer, sales occuring pursuant to a brokers' transaction, the amount of securities sold being within certain volume limitations, and the filing of the notice of resale form. These four requirements do not apply to sales of restricted securities that are made by nonaffiliates, provided at least two years have elapsed between such resale and the security's issuance by the issuer.

7

Recapitalizations, Reorganizations, and Acquisitions

C. Reorganizations Under 3(a)(10)

1. Nonbankruptcy Reorganizations

Page 522. Insert the following at the end of the carryover paragraph at the top of the page.

In 1996, Section 18 of the Securities Act was amended by the National Securities Markets Improvement Act (NSMIA) to exempt "covered securities" from state blue sky laws. As seen in Chapter 4, Section 18 defines covered securities to include not only securities listed on the NYSE and the NASDAQ National Market System but also most items covered by Section 3(a) of the Securities Act, including Section 3(a)(10). Immediately, concern arose over whether NSMIA preempted *all* state fairness hearings related to securities transactions so that no longer could issuers even rely on Section 3(a)(10) to exempt their offerings from Section 5. In 1998, Congress addressed much of this concern by amending Section 18 to remove from the category of covered securities those that are exempt from registration by virtue of Section 3(a)(10). Prior to Congress's action in 1998, the SEC's staff had taken the position that NSMIA did not preempt state fairness proceeding that is not related to the registration of securities. SEC Staff Legal Bulletin No. 3 (July 25, 1997). The staff believed that exemption from federal registration of securities would continue for fairness hearings carried out, for example, by banking and insurance regulatory agencies. A fair reading of newly amended Section 18 suggests that a fairness hearing, carried out by the blue sky administrator to approve the fairness of an exchange being conducted with existing stockholders, is not preempted by Section 18 so that not only does the exemption afforded to the issuer by Section 3(a)(10) apply, but also the state's power to carry out such a hearing is unaffected by Section 18. Is this result consistent with the vision Congress had when it enacted NSMIA?

One further interesting development is the recognition in Related Capital Co., SEC No-Action Letter, [1996 Transfer Binder] Fed. Sec. L. Rep. (CCH) ¶ 77,269 (Sept. 27, 1996), that shares distributed as part of the settlement of a class action fall within the Section 3(a)(10) exemption.

8
Exempt Securities

B. Municipal Securities

6. Rule 15c2-12

Page 555. Insert the following update immediately prior to "Notes and Questions":

Update: Early in 1998, the SEC settled an enforcement action against Credit Suisse First Boston Corp. stemming from a 1994 underwriting of more than $110 million of Orange County bonds. Asserting that the offering statement used in the underwriting misrepresented and omitted material facts, the Commission proceeded against the firm on the theory that the underwriter cannot simply rely on statements from the issuer in determining the adequacy of disclosure. In an interview concerning the settlement reported in *The Wall Street Journal*, the head of the SEC's regional office pointedly commented that underwriters "can't just slap their names on an offering circular [without] a reasonable basis for belief" that the information it contains is accurate. *See* SEC Tightens Disclosure Rules in Settling Orange County Case, Wall St. J., Jan. 30, 1998, at C1. First Boston agreed to pay a fine of $800 thousand to resolve the SEC claims. Subsequently, the firm settled claims brought by the county. *See* Credit Suisse First Boston Settles Orange County Suit for $52.5 Million, 30 BNA Sec. Reg. and Law Report 748 (May 15, 1998).

The Commission also settled an action against Merrill Lynch based on its failure to conduct a professional review of official statements used in Orange County bond offerings underwritten by the firm. The Commission noted that the settlement represents the first time the SEC "has placed blame for misleading disclosure squarely on an underwriter for failing to convey vital information about an offering to the firm's investment bankers." *See* Merrill Agrees to Pay $2 Million in Orange County Settlement with SEC, 30 BNA Sec. Reg. and Law Report 1278 (Aug. 28, 1998). The information not conveyed included the importance of key interest rate assumptions on likely investment returns and potential loss of principal. The settlement followed Merrill's earlier settlement for $400 million of the county's law suit against it.

Among other institutional casualties of the Orange County offerings are accounting firm KPMG Peat Marwick ($75 million settlement) and bond counsel LeBoeuf, Lamb, Greene & MacRae ($55 million settlement). *See* KPMG Peat Marwick Settles Orange County Lawsuits for $75 Million, 30 BNA Sec. Reg. and Law Report 801 (May 22, 1998).

‖9‖
Liability Under the Securities Acts

C. Section 12(a)(2)

1. By Means of a "Prospectus or Oral Communication"

Page 634. Insert the following cases immediately after the *Gustafson* opinion.

Dietrich v. Bauer
Fed. Sec. L. Rep. (CCH) ¶99,411 (S.D.N.Y. 1996)

McKENNA, J. . . . Plaintiff's Section 12(2) claims must also be dismissed because they were not made in relation to a prospectus or initial offering. The Supreme Court recently noted that the courts of appeals "agree that the phrase 'oral communication' is restricted to oral communications that relate to a prospectus." *Gustafson v. Alloyd Co., Inc.,* 513 U.S. 561, 115 S. Ct. 1061, 1066, 131 L. Ed. 2d 1 (1995). . . .

The reasons for limiting actionable oral communications to those that relate to a prospectus are several. First, the 1933 Act was primarily intended to mandate registration and disclosure of certain information with regard to initial public offerings. *Gustafson,* 115 S. Ct. at 1068 (citing *Blue Chip Stamps v. Manor Drug Stores,* 421 U.S. 723, 752, 44 L. Ed. 2d 539, 95 S. Ct. 1917, *reh'g denied,* 423 U.S. 884, 46 L. Ed. 2d 114, 96 S. Ct. 157 (1975) ("The 1933 Act is . . . chiefly concerned with disclosure and fraud in connection with offerings of securities—primarily . . . initial distributions of newly issued stock from corporate issuers."). If oral communications are

37

covered under the 1933 Act, they are only covered to the extent necessary to effectuate the purpose of the Act. Holding actionable oral communications made by brokers and other individuals unconnected with the initial offering, in the secondary market, is not necessary to effectuate the purpose of the 1933 Act.

Second, canons of statutory construction support the finding that the terms "oral communication" and "prospectus" in 15 U.S.C. § 771(2) be read as related terms. *Gustafson*, 115 S. Ct. at 1069 (the doctrine of *noscitur a sociis* provides that a word is known by the company it keeps). The fact that the words "oral communication" in Section 12(2) are directly preceded by the word "prospectus" indicates that the statute should be read so that the word "prospectus" limits the words "oral communication," giving one common reading to the statute rather than multiple antithetical meanings. *Gustafson*, 115 S. Ct. at 1071; *accord Pacific*, 993 F.2d at 588 (the words "oral communication" are words of form, not substance; they describe how one communicates a message, not the message communicated). Conversely, the *Gustafson* Court noted that where the limiting word "prospectus" was not present, as in *United States v. Naftalin*, 441 U.S. 768, 781-82, 60 L. Ed. 2d 624, 99 S.Ct. 2077 (1979), the Court read the language of § 17(a) of the 1933 Act expansively.

Third, the absence in Section 12(2) of the requirement that one prove reliance or fraud can only be explained by the meticulous care with which public offering documents are drafted and the extensive distribution of those documents. *Pollack v. Laidlaw Holdings, Inc.*, 1995 U.S. Dist. LEXIS 5909, 1995 WL 261518 at *15. Holding actionable oral representations not made in connection with these documents creates liability for buyers and sellers in the secondary market where there are different standards governing disclosure. It is not plausible to infer that Congress created this extensive liability for every casual communication between buyer and seller in the secondary market. *Gustafson*, 115 S. Ct. at 1071. For these reasons, agreeing with other courts that have considered this issue, the Court holds actionable under § 12(2) only oral statements made in relation to a prospectus.

Vannest v. Sage, Rutty & Co., Inc.
960 F. Supp. 651 (W.D.N.Y. 1997)

LARIMER, CHIEF J. This case arises out of the sale of limited partnership interests. Plaintiffs purchased interests in a limited partnership formed for the purpose of purchasing a first mortgage on an apartment building. . . .

Shares in the limited partnership were available pursuant to an August 15, 1986 Private Placement Memorandum. . . .

[Plaintiffs alleged fraud and misrepresentations in the sale of the partnership interests.]

A) Plaintiffs' Section 12(2) Claim:

Sage, Rutty asserts that this claim cannot be sustained against it because, as a matter of law, Section 12(2) is applicable to "public" offerings only and this case involves a "private placement" of securities. Sage, Rutty relies on *Gustafson v. Alloyd Co., Inc.* There, the Supreme Court determined that "prospectus" as used in Section 12(2) is a document used only in a public offering of securities by an issuer or controlling shareholder. . . .

Sage, Rutty asserts that this case is controlled by Gustafson because the securities here were purchased through a Private Placement Memorandum. Plaintiffs assert that since *Gustafson*, courts routinely have dismissed Section 12(2) claims based upon statements made in private placement memoranda. *See Lennon v. Christoph*, 1996 U.S. Dist. LEXIS 9943, *52 (N.D. Ill. 1996); *Glamorgan Coal Corp. v. Ratner's Group, P.L.C.*, 1995 U.S. Dist. LEXIS 9548, 1995 WL 406167 (S.D.N.Y. July 1995).

Plaintiffs counter that Sage, Rutty has the burden of proving that the transaction was not a public offering, and that in order not to be a public offering, the transaction must have certain characteristics such as the number of offerees, the offerees' sophistication, the size and manner of the offering and the issuer's relationship to the offerees. *See Koehler v. Pulvers*, 614 F. Supp. 829 (S.D. Cal. 1985). At oral argument, plaintiffs further asserted that the criteria set forth in the Security and Exchange Commission's Rule 506 of Regulation D (concerning the number of purchasers and their sophistication) must be met to qualify as a private offering. Thus, plaintiffs assert that a material issue of fact exists as to whether the transactions at issue in this case are public or private offerings.

The *Gustafson* decision has been criticized for making a complex area of law even more confusing. *See, e.g.*, Janet E. Kerr, Ralston Redux: Determining Which Section 3 Offerings are Public under Section 12(2) after *Gustafson*, 50 SMU L. Rev. 175 (1996); Stephen M. Bainbridge, Securities Act Section 12(2) After the *Gustafson* Debacle, 50 Bus. Law. 1231 (1995); Elliott J. Weiss, Securities Act Section 12(2) After *Gustafson v. Alloyd Co.*: What Questions Remain?, 50 Bus. Law. 1209 (1995). The Supreme Court's simple conclusion that Section 12(2) applies only to public offerings does not make the process of determining what is and is not a public offering any simpler. As one commentator has found, the *Gustafson* court's attempt to equate public offerings with those that are registered ignores the important fact that not all public offerings are registered. Kerr, 50 SMU L. Rev. at 187-188. The complex relationship of statutory and regulatory provisions that comprises the federal securities laws insures that determining whether an offer is public, in the shadow of *Gustafson*, is more complex than ever.

Since *Gustafson*, some courts addressing the issue have determined that, by definition, offerings made via a private placement memorandum are not public offerings. *See In re J.W.P. Inc. Securities Litigation*, 928 F. Supp. 1239, 1259 (S.D.N.Y. 1996) ("Courts in this district have held that under

Gustafson, private placement memoranda like those at issue are not 'prospectuses' for the purposes of a claim under § 12(2)"); *Glamorgan Coal Corp.,* 1995 U.S. Dist. LEXIS 9548 at *2-*3, 1995 WL at *2-*3 (offering made by private placement memorandum not public for Section 12(2) purposes); *see also Whirlpool Financial Corp. v. GN Holdings, Inc.,* 67 F.3d 605, 609, n.2 (7th Cir. 1995), *reh'g denied,* (where the court noted that because a 'prospectus' for Section 12(2) purposes includes only public offerings, Section 12(2) claims arising from sale of securities offered through a private placement memorandum had been properly dismissed).

Other courts have ruled otherwise. *See Fisk v. SuperAnnuities, Inc.,* 927 F. Supp. 718 (S.D.N.Y. 1996) (where the court refused to dismiss Section 12(2) claims even where securities were offered via private placement memorandum where plaintiffs contended that offering was not truly private); *but cf., ESI Montgomery County, Inc. v. Montenay Intern. Corp.,* 899 F. Supp. 1061 (S.D.N.Y. 1995) (where court dismissed Section 12(2) claims where plaintiff acknowledged the offering was made by private offering memoranda, but noted that "had plaintiff alleged that the offering was public it would be premature for the court to assess the weight of [the factors for determining whether an offering is public]").

In this case the PPM expressly (and repeatedly) states that the offering is not subject to registration requirements and that the securities are intended to be sold only to purchasers qualified by the Rule 506 regulations. Clearly the drafters contemplated a private offering.

The plaintiffs have never asserted a Section 12(1) claim—for registration violations—and they do not dispute that the offering was made pursuant to a private placement memorandum. Although plaintiffs now claim that the offering was not truly a private offering, this assertion, which is made for the first time six years after the complaint was filed, is not compelling. It is evident to me that until *Gustafson* plaintiffs never seriously contested the private nature of the offering at issue.

Thus, based upon my analysis of the facts in this case, I choose to follow the reasoning of the *J.W.P. Inc. Securities Litigation* and the *Glamorgan* cases. I find that because the Pfeiffer House offering was made by a Private Placement Memorandum, and because the stated intent at the time was to characterize the offering as private, it was not a "public" offering. Because Section 12(2) is inapplicable to private offerings under *Gustafson,* plaintiffs' Section 12(2) claim against Sage, Rutty is dismissed. . . .

11
Fraud in Connection with the Purchase or Sale of a Security

A. What is Proscribed By Rule 10b-5

1. Fraud "In Connection with" the Purchase or Sale of a Security

b. The "In Connection with" Requirement at the Margins

Page 690. Add at the end of the first paragraph:

Two court of appeals decisions have made clear that for fraud to be "in connection with," it need not relate to the value of the security in question. In *SEC v. Jakubowski*, 150 F.3d 675 (7th Cir. 1998), the court found the requirement as satisfied in a case where an attorney allegedly made false statements as to the identity of the purchasers of the stock of a converted savings and loan institution. The court stated that any doubt over the issue was removed by the Supreme Court's endorsement of the misappropriation theory of insider trading liability in *United States v. O'Hagan* (*see* Chapter 12 infra), wherein the deception relates to the fiduciary misconduct of the trader. A similar rejection of the "value" dicta can be found in *Press v. Chemical Investment Services Corp.*, 166 F.3d 529 (2d Cir. 1999) (misrepresentation regarding investor's access to the security upon maturity).

❚❙ Page 741.   11.   Fraud in Connection with the Purchase/Sale of a Security   ❙❚

B.   Private Rights of Action Under Rule 10b-5

2.   Pleading Fraud

Page 741.   Add the following at the end of Note 1:

In the aftermath of the Reform Act, courts have struggled with the proper interpretation of the new pleading standard's "strong inference" requirement. Two contentious issues have emerged. The first is whether the Second Circuit's approach, allowing a "motive and opportunity" story to be told as a way of establishing the inference, survives. *Compare Rehm v. Eagle Fin. Corp.*, 954 F. Supp. 1246 (N.D. Ill. 1997) (yes) *with In re Silicon Graphics Inc. Sec. Lit.*, 970 F. Supp. 746 (N.D. Cal. 1997) (no).

The second issue is whether pleading circumstantial evidence of recklessness suffices, or whether that evidence must create a strong inference of knowing or intentional misconduct. *Silicon Graphics* is among the cases rejecting recklessness. *Compare In re Baesa Sec. Lit.*, 969 F. Supp. 238 (S.D.N.Y. 1997).

An effort to resolve this tension was made in the legislative history (but not the text) of the Securities Litigation Uniform Standards Act of 1998. The Statement of Managers, accompanied by a discussion among certain key members on the floor, was designed—apparently at the behest of the SEC—to state that Congress's intent in 1995 was fully consistent with the Second Circuit's "motive and opportunity" and "recklessness" standards. While many of the statements in the legislative history indeed support this view, however, some members of Congress appeared to disagree. Moreover, it may be open to question whether a subsequent Congress can without legislation attach a meaning to a previously enacted statute. Hence, although the 1998 Act certainly gives support to the more permissive construction of the pleading requirement, it may not resolve the dispute.

Much ink has been spilled on the question of whether the pleading standard, if construed strictly, makes it unreasonably difficult to bring meritorious cases. An interesting article, Weiss & Moser, *Enter Yossarian: How to Resolve the Procedural Catch-22 That the Private Securities Litigation Reform Act Creates*, 76 Wash. U.L.Q. 457 (1998), explores this by reference to an actual case study. In late 1997, Green Tree Financial made an announcement that it would increase its loan loss and prepayment reserves by a considerable amount, causing an immediate and significant stock price drop. Class action fraud-on-the-market suits were immediately filed. A few months later, the company essentially conceded many facts that gave support to plaintiffs' claims. What the authors do is imagine that the company had not made the later concessions. Would the facts available when the

■| 11. **Fraud in Connection with the Purchase/Sale of a Security   Page 741.** |■

actions were first filed have been enough to survive a motion to dismiss? If not, then this would be an example of a meritorious action that would have floundered on pleading grounds alone. Weiss and Moser claim that it would have been easy to dismiss the case and recommend that courts avoid such an impact by granting limited discovery in cases that establish plausible grounds for fraud in order to enable plaintiffs to reach the level of "strong inference."

12

The Regulation of Insider Trading

B. The Source of a Duty to Abstain or Disclose

Page 782. Add to the end of Note 5:

Two courts of appeals have disagreed with *Teicher* and held that "misuse" of information is a necessary element of an insider trading action under Rule 10b-5. In *SEC v. Adler*, 137 F.3d 1325 (11th Cir. 1998), an insider twice allegedly sold stock while in possession of bad news about his company's financial condition. He argued with respect to one of the sales that he had already made plans to sell his stock, in part because he needed the money to purchase an eighteen-wheel truck for his son. Citing a variety of sources (including much dicta from Supreme Court decisions, such as *Chiarella*), the court agreed that there is no violation of Rule 10b-5 when there is no causal connection between the receipt of the information and the subsequent trading. However, it determined that a showing of possession raises a "strong inference" of misuse so that the burden shifts to the defendant to negate causation. Applying this standard, the court reversed the district court's grant of summary judgment for the defendant in the case, finding it at least a triable issue of fact as to whether the defendant could overcome the presumption.

In *United States v. Smith*, 155 F.3d 1051 (9th Cir. 1998), the Ninth Circuit followed *Adler's* insistence upon a showing of misuse. Because it was a criminal prosecution under Rule 10b-5, however, the court rejected the idea that possession should lead to a presumption of misuse, thus leaving the entire burden of showing scienter on the prosecutors. The court took no position on the question of whether the presumption would be appropriate in a civil case.

F. The Misappropriation Theory

Page 800. Replace the *Bryan* case with the following:

United States v. O'Hagan
117 S. Ct. 2199 (1997)

GINSBURG, J. This case concerns the interpretation and enforcement of Section 10(b) and Section 14(e) of the Securities Exchange Act of 1934, and rules made by the Securities and Exchange Commission pursuant to these provisions, Rule 10b-5 and Rule 14e-3(a). Two prime questions are presented. The first relates to the misappropriation of material, nonpublic information for securities trading; the second concerns fraudulent practices in the tender offer setting. In particular, we address and resolve these issues: (1) Is a person who trades in securities for personal profit, using confidential information misappropriated in breach of a fiduciary duty to the source of the information, guilty of violating Section 10(b) and Rule 10b-5? (2) Did the Commission exceed its rulemaking authority by adopting Rule 14e-3(a), which proscribes trading on undisclosed information in the tender offer setting, even in the absence of a duty to disclose? Our answer to the first question is yes, and to the second question, viewed in the context of this case, no.

I

Respondent James Herman O'Hagan was a partner in the law firm of Dorsey & Whitney in Minneapolis, Minnesota. In July 1988, Grand Metropolitan PLC (Grand Met), a company based in London, England, retained Dorsey & Whitney as local counsel to represent Grand Met regarding a potential tender offer for the common stock of the Pillsbury Company, headquartered in Minneapolis. Both Grand Met and Dorsey & Whitney took precautions to protect the confidentiality of Grand Met's tender offer plans. O'Hagan did no work on the Grand Met representation. Dorsey & Whitney withdrew from representing Grand Met on September 9, 1988. Less than a month later, on October 4, 1988, Grand Met publicly announced its tender offer for Pillsbury stock.

On August 18, 1988, while Dorsey & Whitney was still representing Grand Met, O'Hagan began purchasing call options for Pillsbury stock.

Each option gave him the right to purchase 100 shares of Pillsbury stock by a specified date in September 1988. Later in August and in September, O'Hagan made additional purchases of Pillsbury call options. By the end of September, he owned 2,500 unexpired Pillsbury options, apparently more than any other individual investor. O'Hagan also purchased, in September 1988, some 5,000 shares of Pillsbury common stock, at a price just under $39 per share. When Grand Met announced its tender offer in October, the price of Pillsbury stock rose to nearly $60 per share. O'Hagan then sold his Pillsbury call options and common stock, making a profit of more than $4.3 million.

The Securities and Exchange Commission initiated an investigation into O'Hagan's transactions, culminating in a 57-count indictment. The indictment alleged that O'Hagan defrauded his law firm and its client, Grand Met, by using for his own trading purposes material, nonpublic information regarding Grand Met's planned tender offer. According to the indictment, O'Hagan used the profits he gained through this trading to conceal his previous embezzlement and conversion of unrelated client trust funds.... A jury convicted O'Hagan on all 57 counts, and he was sentenced to a 41-month term of imprisonment.

A divided panel of the Court of Appeals for the Eighth Circuit reversed all of O'Hagan's convictions. 92 F.3d 612 (1996). Liability under Section 10(b) and Rule 10b-5, the Eighth Circuit held, may not be grounded on the "misappropriation theory" of securities fraud on which the prosecution relied. Id. at 622. The Court of Appeals also held that Rule 14e-3(a)—which prohibits trading while in possession of material, nonpublic information relating to a tender offer—exceeds the SEC's Section 14(e) rulemaking authority because the rule contains no breach of fiduciary duty requirement. Id. at 627....

Decisions of the Courts of Appeals are in conflict on the propriety of the misappropriation theory under Section 10(b) and Rule 10b-5, and on the legitimacy of Rule 14e-3(a) under Section 14(e). We granted certiorari, and now reverse the Eighth Circuit's judgment.

II

We address first the Court of Appeals' reversal of O'Hagan's convictions under Section 10(b) and Rule 10b-5. Following the Fourth Circuit's lead, *see United States v. Bryan*, 58 F.3d 933, 943-959 (1995), the Eighth Circuit rejected the misappropriation theory as a basis for Section 10(b) liability. We hold, in accord with several other Courts of Appeals, that

■ I Page 800. 12. The Regulation of Insider Trading I ■

criminal liability under Section 10(b) may be predicated on the misappropriation theory[4]....

A

[Section 10(b)] proscribes (1) using any deceptive device (2) in connection with the purchase or sale of securities, in contravention of rules prescribed by the Commission. The provision, as written, does not confine its coverage to deception of a purchaser or seller of securities, *see United States v. Newman*, 664 F.2d 12, 17 (CA2 1981); rather, the statute reaches any deceptive device used "in connection with the purchase or sale of any security...."

The "misappropriation theory" holds that a person commits fraud "in connection with" a securities transaction, and thereby violates Section 10(b) and Rule 10b-5, when he misappropriates confidential information for securities trading purposes, in breach of a duty owed to the source of the information. Under this theory, a fiduciary's undisclosed, self-serving use of a principal's information to purchase or sell securities, in breach of a duty of loyalty and confidentiality, defrauds the principal of the exclusive use of that information. In lieu of premising liability on a fiduciary relationship between company insider and purchaser or seller of the company's stock, the misappropriation theory premises liability on a fiduciary-turned-trader's deception of those who entrusted him with access to confidential information.... The misappropriation theory is thus designed to "protect the integrity of the securities markets against abuses by 'outsiders' to a corporation who have access to confidential information that will affect the corporation's security price when revealed, but who owe no fiduciary or other duty to that corporation's shareholders" [quoting *Dirks v. SEC*, 463 U.S. 646, 655 (1983)].

In this case, the indictment alleged that O'Hagan, in breach of a duty of trust and confidence he owed to his law firm, Dorsey & Whitney, and

---

4. Twice before we have been presented with the question whether criminal liability for violation of Section 10(b) may be based on a misappropriation theory. In Chiarella v. United States, 445 U.S. 222 (1980), the jury had received no misappropriation theory instructions, so we declined to address the question. In Carpenter v. United States, 484 U.S. 19 (1987), the Court divided evenly on whether, under the circumstances of that case, convictions resting on the misappropriation theory should be affirmed. *See* Aldave, The Misappropriation Theory: *Carpenter* and Its Aftermath, 49 Ohio St. L.J. 373, 375 (1988) (observing that "*Carpenter* was, by any reckoning, an unusual case," for the information there misappropriated belonged not to a company preparing to engage in securities transactions, *e.g.*, a bidder in a corporate acquisition, but to The Wall Street Journal).

to its client, Grand Met, traded on the basis of nonpublic information regarding Grand Met's planned tender offer for Pillsbury common stock. This conduct, the Government charged, constituted a fraudulent device in connection with the purchase and sale of securities.

B

We agree with the Government that misappropriation, as just defined, satisfies Section 10(b)'s requirement that chargeable conduct involve a "deceptive device or contrivance" used "in connection with" the purchase or sale of securities. We observe, first, that misappropriators, as the Government describes them, deal in deception. A fiduciary who "[pretends] loyalty to the principal while secretly converting the principal's information for personal gain," Brief for United States 17, "dupes" or defrauds the principal. . . .

Deception through nondisclosure is central to the theory of liability for which the Government seeks recognition. As counsel for the Government stated in explanation of the theory at oral argument: "To satisfy the common law rule that a trustee may not use the property that [has] been entrusted [to] him, there would have to be consent. To satisfy the requirement of the Securities Act that there be no deception, there would only have to be disclosure."

The misappropriation theory advanced by the Government is consistent with *Santa Fe Industries, Inc. v. Green*, 430 U.S. 462 (1977), a decision underscoring that Section 10(b) is not an all-purpose breach of fiduciary duty ban; rather, it trains on conduct involving manipulation or deception. In contrast to the Government's allegations in this case, in *Santa Fe Industries*, all pertinent facts were disclosed by the persons charged with violating Section 10(b) and Rule 10b-5; therefore, there was no deception through nondisclosure to which liability under those provisions could attach. Similarly, full disclosure forecloses liability under the misappropriation theory: Because the deception essential to the misappropriation theory involves feigning fidelity to the source of information, if the fiduciary discloses to the source that he plans to trade on the nonpublic information, there is no "deceptive device" and thus no Section 10(b) violation—although the fiduciary-turned-trader may remain liable under state law for breach of a duty of loyalty.

We turn next to the Section 10(b) requirement that the misappropriator's deceptive use of information be "in connection with the purchase or sale of [a] security." This element is satisfied because the fiduciary's fraud is consummated, not when the fiduciary gains the confidential information, but when, without disclosure to his principal, he uses the information to purchase or sell securities. The securities transaction and the breach of duty thus coincide. This is so even though the person or entity defrauded is not the other party to the trade, but is, instead, the source of the nonpublic information. A misappropriator who trades on the basis of material, nonpublic information, in short, gains his advantageous market position through deception; he deceives the source of the information and simultaneously harms members of the investing public.

The misappropriation theory targets information of a sort that misappropriators ordinarily capitalize upon to gain no-risk profits through the purchase or sale of securities. Should a misappropriator put such information to other use, the statute's prohibition would not be implicated. The theory does not catch all conceivable forms of fraud involving confidential information; rather, it catches fraudulent means of capitalizing on such information through securities transactions.... [At this point, the Court dealt with the concern expressed in the dissent of Justice Thomas, infra, that misappropriation is not securities fraud because the misappropriation of information does not necessarily result in securities trading. The majority responded that it was enough that such misappropriation "ordinarily" results in a securities trade.]

The misappropriation theory comports with Section 10(b)'s language, which requires deception "in connection with the purchase or sale of any security," not deception of an identifiable purchaser or seller. The theory is also well-tuned to an animating purpose of the Exchange Act: to insure honest securities markets and thereby promote investor confidence. *See* 45 Fed. Reg. 60412 (1980) (trading on misappropriated information "undermines the integrity of, and investor confidence in, the securities markets"). Although informational disparity is inevitable in the securities markets, investors likely would hesitate to venture their capital in a market where trading based on misappropriated nonpublic information is unchecked by law. An investor's informational disadvantage vis-à-vis a misappropriator with material, nonpublic information stems from contrivance, not luck; it is a disadvantage that cannot be overcome with research or skill. *See* Brudney, Insiders, Outsiders, and Informational Advantages Under the Federal Securities Laws, 93 Harv. L. Rev. 322, 356 (1979) ("If the market is thought to be systematically populated with ... transactors [trading on the basis of misappropriated information] some investors will refrain from dealing altogether, and others will incur costs to avoid dealing with such transactors or corruptly to overcome their unerodable informational advantages.").

. . .

In sum, considering the inhibiting impact on market participation of trading on misappropriated information, and the congressional purposes underlying Section 10(b), it makes scant sense to hold a lawyer like O'Hagan a Section 10(b) violator if he works for a law firm representing the target of a tender offer, but not if he works for a law firm representing the bidder.

The text of the statute requires no such result.[9] The misappropriation at issue here was properly made the subject of a Section 10(b) charge because it meets the statutory requirement that there be "deceptive" conduct "in connection with" securities transactions. . . .

[The Court then went on to show that its previous decisions did not compel a rejection of the misappropriation theory. Having found the theory consistent with text, policy and precedent, it remanded to the lower court for further proceedings on O'Hagan's other defenses to liability.]

III

We consider next the ground on which the Court of Appeals reversed O'Hagan's convictions for fraudulent trading in connection with a tender offer, in violation of Section 14(e) of the Exchange Act and SEC Rule 14e-3(a). A sole question is before us as to these convictions: Did the Commission, as the Court of Appeals held, exceed its rulemaking authority under Section 14(e) when it adopted Rule 14e-3(a) without requiring a showing that the trading at issue entailed a breach of fiduciary duty? We hold that the Commission, in this regard and to the extent relevant to this case, did not exceed its authority.

The governing statutory provision, Section 14(e) of the Exchange Act, reads in relevant part:

> It shall be unlawful for any person . . . to engage in any fraudulent, deceptive, or manipulative acts or practices, in connection with any tender offer. . . . The [SEC] shall, for the purposes of this subsection, by rules and regulations define, and prescribe means reasonably designed to prevent, such acts and practices as are fraudulent, deceptive, or manipulative.
> 15 U.S.C. section 78n(e).

---

9. As noted earlier, however, the textual requirement of deception precludes Section 10(b) liability when a person trading on the basis of nonpublic information has disclosed his trading plans to, or obtained authorization from, the principal—even though such conduct may affect the securities markets in the same manner as the conduct reached by the misappropriation theory. Contrary to the dissent's suggestion, the fact that Section 10(b) is only a partial antidote to the problems it was designed to alleviate does not call into question its prohibition of conduct that falls within its textual proscription. Moreover, once a disloyal agent discloses his imminent breach of duty, his principal may seek appropriate equitable relief under state law. Furthermore, in the context of a tender offer, the principal who authorizes an agent's trading on confidential information may, in the Commission's view, incur liability for an Exchange Act violation under Rule 14e-3(a).

As characterized by the Commission, Rule 14e-3(a) is a "disclose or abstain from trading" requirement. 45 Fed. Reg. 60410 (1980). The Second Circuit concisely described the rule's thrust:

> One violates Rule 14e-3(a) if he trades on the basis of material nonpublic information concerning a pending tender offer that he knows or has reason to know has been acquired 'directly or indirectly' from an insider of the offeror or issuer, or someone working on their behalf. Rule 14e-3(a) is a disclosure provision. It creates a duty in those traders who fall within its ambit to abstain or disclose, without regard to whether the trader owes a pre-existing fiduciary duty to respect the confidentiality of the information.

United States v. Chestman, 947 F.2d 551, 557 (1991) (en banc), *cert. denied,* 503 U.S. 1004 (1992).

The Eighth Circuit homed in on the essence of Section 14(e)'s rulemaking authorization: "The statute empowers the SEC to 'define' and 'prescribe means reasonably designed to prevent' 'acts and practices' which are 'fraudulent.'" All that means, the Eighth Circuit found plain, is that the SEC may "identify and regulate," in the tender offer context, "acts and practices" the law already defines as "fraudulent"; but, the Eighth Circuit maintained, the SEC may not "create its own definition of fraud . . . As to the Commission's Section 14(e) authority to "prescribe means reasonably designed to prevent" fraudulent acts, the Eighth Circuit stated: "Properly read, this provision means simply that the SEC has broad regulatory powers in the field of tender offers, but the statutory terms have a fixed meaning which the SEC cannot alter by way of an administrative rule." 92 F.3d at 627.

The United States urges that the Eighth Circuit's reading of Section 14(e) misapprehends both the Commission's authority to define fraudulent acts and the Commission's power to prevent them. "The 'defining' power," the United States submits, "would be a virtual nullity were the SEC not permitted to go beyond common law fraud (which is separately prohibited in the first [self-operative] sentence of Section 14(e))." . . .

We need not resolve in this case whether the Commission's authority under Section 14(e) to "define . . . such acts and practices as are fraudulent" is broader than the Commission's fraud-defining authority under Section 10(b), for we agree with the United States that Rule 14e-3(a), as applied to cases of this genre, qualifies under Section 14(e) as a "means reasonably designed to prevent" fraudulent trading on material, nonpublic information in the tender offer context.[17] A prophylactic measure, because its

---

17. We leave for another day, when the issue requires decision, the legitimacy of Rule 14e-3(a) as applied to "warehousing," which the Government describes as "the practice by which bidders leak advance information of a tender offer to allies and encourage them to purchase the target company's stock before the bid is announced." As we observed in *Chiarella,* one of the Commission's purposes in proposing Rule 14e-3(a) was "to bar warehousing under its authority to regulate

mission is to prevent, typically encompasses more than the core activity prohibited. . . .

In adopting the "disclose or abstain" rule, the SEC explained:

> The Commission has previously expressed and continues to have serious concerns about trading by persons in possession of material, nonpublic information relating to a tender offer. This practice results in unfair disparities in market information and market disruption. Security holders who purchase from or sell to such persons are effectively denied the benefits of disclosure and the substantive protections of the Williams Act. If furnished with the information, these security holders would be able to make an informed investment decision, which could involve deferring the purchase or sale of the securities until the material information had been disseminated or until the tender offer has been commenced or terminated.
> 45 Fed. Reg. 60412 (1980) (footnotes omitted).

The Commission thus justified Rule 14e-3(a) as a means necessary and proper to assure the efficacy of Williams Act protections.

The United States emphasizes that Rule 14e-3(a) reaches trading in which "a breach of duty is likely but difficult to prove." "Particularly in the context of a tender offer," as the Tenth Circuit recognized, "there is a fairly wide circle of people with confidential information," [*SEC v. Peters*, 978 F.2d 1162, 1167 (10th Cir. 1992)], notably, the attorneys, investment bankers, and accountants involved in structuring the transaction. The availability of that information may lead to abuse, for "even a hint of an upcoming tender offer may send the price of the target company's stock soaring." *SEC v. Materia*, 745 F.2d 197, 199 (2d Cir. 1984). Individuals entrusted with nonpublic information, particularly if they have no long-term loyalty to the issuer, may find the temptation to trade on that information hard to resist in view of "the very large short-term profits potentially available [to them]." *Peters*, 978 F.2d at 1167.

"It may be possible to prove circumstantially that a person [traded on the basis of material, nonpublic information], but almost impossible to prove that the trader obtained such information in breach of a fiduciary duty owed either by the trader or by the ultimate insider source of the information." Ibid. The example of a "tippee" who trades on information received from an insider illustrates the problem. Under Rule 10b-5, "a tippee assumes a fiduciary duty to the shareholders of a corporation not to trade on material nonpublic information only when the insider has

---

tender offers." 445 U.S. at 234. The Government acknowledges that trading authorized by a principal breaches no fiduciary duty. The instant case, however, does not involve trading authorized by a principal; therefore, we need not here decide whether the Commission's proscription of warehousing falls within its Section 14(e) authority to define or prevent fraud.

breached his fiduciary duty to the shareholders by disclosing the information to the tippee and the tippee knows or should know that there has been a breach." *Dirks,* 463 U.S. at 660. To show that a tippee who traded on nonpublic information about a tender offer had breached a fiduciary duty would require proof not only that the insider source breached a fiduciary duty, but that the tippee knew or should have known of that breach. "Yet, in most cases, the only parties to the [information transfer] will be the insider and the alleged tippee." *Peters,* 978 F.2d at 1167.[20]

In sum, it is a fair assumption that trading on the basis of material, nonpublic information will often involve a breach of a duty of confidentiality to the bidder or target company or their representatives. The SEC, cognizant of the proof problem that could enable sophisticated traders to escape responsibility, placed in Rule 14e-3(a) a "disclose or abstain from trading" command that does not require specific proof of a breach of fiduciary duty[21].... Therefore, insofar as it serves to prevent the type of misappropriation charged against O'Hagan, Rule 14e-3(a) is a proper exercise of the Commission's prophylactic power under Section 14(e)....

The judgment of the Court of Appeals for the Eighth Circuit is reversed, and the case is remanded for further proceedings consistent with this opinion.

[The concurring and dissenting opinion of Justice SCALIA is omitted.]

Justice THOMAS, with whom Chief Justice REHNQUIST joins, concurring in the judgment in part and dissenting in part.

Today the majority upholds respondent's convictions for violating Section 10(b) of the Securities Exchange Act of 1934, and Rule 10b-5 promulgated thereunder, based upon the Securities and Exchange Commission's "misappropriation theory." Central to the majority's holding is the need to interpret Section 10(b)'s requirement that a deceptive device be "used or employed, in connection with the purchase or sale of any security." Because the Commission's misappropriation theory fails to provide a coherent and consistent interpretation of this essential requirement for liability under Section 10(b), I dissent.

---

20. The dissent opines that there is no reason to anticipate difficulties in proving breach of duty in "misappropriation" cases. "Once the source of the [purloined] information has been identified," the dissent asserts, "it should be a simple task to obtain proof of any breach of duty." To test that assertion, assume a misappropriating partner at Dorsey & Whitney told his daughter or son and a wealthy friend that a tender for Pillsbury was in the offing, and each tippee promptly purchased Pillsbury stock, the child borrowing the purchase price from the wealthy friend. The dissent's confidence, that "there is no reason to suspect that the tipper would gratuitously protect the tippee," seems misplaced.

21. The dissent insists that even if the misappropriation of information from the bidder about a tender offer is fraud, the Commission has not explained why such fraud is "in connection with" a tender offer. What else, one can only wonder, might such fraud be "in connection with"?

I

I do not take issue with the majority's determination that the undisclosed misappropriation of confidential information by a fiduciary can constitute a "deceptive device" within the meaning of Section 10(b).... Unlike the majority, however, I cannot accept the Commission's interpretation of when a deceptive device is "used . . . in connection with" a securities transaction. Although the Commission and the majority at points seem to suggest that any relation to a securities transaction satisfies the "in connection with" requirement of Section 10(b), both ultimately reject such an overly expansive construction and require a more integral connection between the fraud and the securities transaction. The majority states, for example, that the misappropriation theory applies to undisclosed misappropriation of confidential information "for securities trading purposes," thus seeming to require a particular intent by the misappropriator in order to satisfy the "in connection with" language. The Commission goes further, and argues that the misappropriation theory satisfies the "in connection with" requirement because it "depends on an inherent connection between the deceptive conduct and the purchase or sale of a security." . . .

The Commission's construction of the relevant language in Section 10(b), and the incoherence of that construction, become evident as the majority attempts to describe why the fraudulent theft of information falls under the Commission's misappropriation theory, but the fraudulent theft of money does not. The majority correctly notes that confidential information "qualifies as property to which the company has a right of exclusive use." It then observes that the "undisclosed misappropriation of such information, in violation of a fiduciary duty . . . constitutes fraud akin to embezzlement—the fraudulent appropriation to one's own use of the money or goods entrusted to one's care by another." So far the majority's analogy to embezzlement is well taken, and adequately demonstrates that undisclosed misappropriation can be a fraud on the source of the information. . . . What the embezzlement analogy does not do, however, is explain how the relevant fraud is "used or employed, in connection with" a securities transaction. And when the majority seeks to distinguish the embezzlement of funds from the embezzlement of information, it becomes clear that neither the Commission nor the majority has a coherent theory regarding Section 10(b)'s "in connection with" requirement. . . .

Accepting the Government's description of the scope of its own theory, it becomes plain that the majority's explanation of how the misappropriation theory supposedly satisfies the "in connection with" requirement is incomplete. The touchstone required for an embezzlement to be "used or employed, in connection with" a securities transaction is not merely that it "coincide" with, or be consummated by, the transaction, but that it is necessarily and only consummated by the transaction. Where the property being embezzled has value "apart from [its] use in a securities transaction"—even though it is in fact being used in a securities transaction—the Government contends that there is no violation under the misappropriation theory.

My understanding of the Government's proffered theory of liability, and its construction of the "in connection with" requirement, is confirmed by the Government's explanation during oral argument:

"[Court]: What if I appropriate some of my client's money in order to buy stock?

. . .

"[Court]: Have I violated the securities laws?

"[Counsel]: I do not think that you have.

"[Court]: Why not? Isn't that in connection with the purchase of securities just as much as this one is?

"[Counsel]: It's not just as much as this one is, because in this case it is the use of the information that enables the profits, pure and simple. There would be no opportunity to engage in profit—

"[Court]: Same here. I didn't have the money. The only way I could buy this stock was to get the money.

. . .

"[Counsel]: The difference . . . is that once you have the money you can do anything you want with it. In a sense, the fraud is complete at that point, and then you go on and you can use the money to finance any number of other activities, but the connection is far less close than in this case, where the only value of this information for personal profit for respondent was to take it and profit in the securities markets by trading on it.

. . .

"[Court]: So what you're saying is, is in this case the misappropriation can only be of relevance, or is of substantial relevance, is with reference to the purchase of securities.

"[Counsel]: Exactly.

"[Court]: When you take money out of the accounts you can go to the racetrack, or whatever.

"[Counsel]: That's exactly right, and because of that difference, [there] can be no doubt that this kind of misappropriation of property is in connection with the purchase or sale of securities. . . .

As the above exchange demonstrates, the relevant distinction is not that the misappropriated information was used for a securities transaction (the money example met that test), but rather that it could only be used for such a transaction. . . .

Once the Government's construction of the misappropriation theory is accurately described and accepted—along with its implied construction of Section 10(b)'s "in connection with" language—that theory should no longer cover cases, such as this one, involving fraud on the source of information where the source has no connection with the other participant

12. The Regulation of Insider Trading   Page 800.

in a securities transaction. It seems obvious that the undisclosed misappropriation of confidential information is not necessarily consummated by a securities transaction. In this case, for example, upon learning of Grand Met's confidential takeover plans, O'Hagan could have done any number of things with the information: He could have sold it to a newspaper for publication, he could have given or sold the information to Pillsbury itself, or he could even have kept the information and used it solely for his personal amusement, perhaps in a fantasy stock trading game.

Any of these activities would have deprived Grand Met of its right to "exclusive use," of the information and, if undisclosed, would constitute "embezzlement" of Grand Met's informational property. Under any theory of liability, however, these activities would not violate Section 10(b) and, according to the Commission's monetary embezzlement analogy, these possibilities are sufficient to preclude a violation under the misappropriation theory even where the informational property was used for securities trading. That O'Hagan actually did use the information to purchase securities is thus no more significant here than it is in the case of embezzling money used to purchase securities. In both cases the embezzler could have done something else with the property, and hence the Commission's necessary "connection" under the securities laws would not be met. If the relevant test under the "in connection with" language is whether the fraudulent act is necessarily tied to a securities transaction, then the misappropriation of confidential information used to trade no more violates Section 10(b) than does the misappropriation of funds used to trade. As the Commission concedes that the latter is not covered under its theory, I am at a loss to see how the same theory can coherently be applied to the former....

In upholding respondent's convictions under the new and improved misappropriation theory, the majority also points to various policy considerations underlying the securities laws, such as maintaining fair and honest markets, promoting investor confidence, and protecting the integrity of the securities markets. But the repeated reliance on such broad-sweeping legislative purposes reaches too far and is misleading in the context of the misappropriation theory. It reaches too far in that, regardless of the overarching purpose of the securities laws, it is not illegal to run afoul of the "purpose" of a statute, only its letter. The majority's approach is misleading in this case because it glosses over the fact that the supposed threat to fair and honest markets, investor confidence, and market integrity comes not from the supposed fraud in this case, but from the mere fact that the information used by O'Hagan was nonpublic.

As the majority concedes, because "the deception essential to the misappropriation theory involves feigning fidelity to the source of information, if the fiduciary discloses to the source that he plans to trade on the nonpublic information, there is no 'deceptive device' and thus no Section

10(b) violation." Indeed, were the source expressly to authorize its agents to trade on the confidential information—as a perk or bonus, perhaps—there would likewise be no Section 10(b) violation. Yet in either case—disclosed misuse or authorized use—the hypothesized "inhibiting impact on market participation," would be identical to that from behavior violating the misappropriation theory: "Outsiders" would still be trading based on nonpublic information that the average investor has no hope of obtaining through his own diligence.[6]

The majority's statement that a "misappropriator who trades on the basis of material, nonpublic information, in short, gains his advantageous market position through deception; he deceives the source of the information and simultaneously harms members of the investing public," thus focuses on the wrong point. Even if it is true that trading on nonpublic information hurts the public, it is true whether or not there is any deception of the source of the information.[7] Moreover, as we have repeatedly held, use of nonpublic information to trade is not itself a violation of Section 10(b). Rather, it is the use of fraud "in connection with" a securities transaction that is forbidden. Where the relevant element of fraud has no impact on the integrity of the subsequent transactions as distinct from the non-fraudulent element of using nonpublic information, one can reasonably question whether the fraud was used in connection with a securities transaction. And one can likewise question whether removing that aspect of fraud, though perhaps laudable, has anything to do with the confidence or integrity of the market. . . .

---

6. That the dishonesty aspect of misappropriation might be eliminated via disclosure or authorization is wholly besides the point. The dishonesty in misappropriation is in the relationship between the fiduciary and the principal, not in any relationship between the misappropriator and the market. No market transaction is made more or less honest by disclosure to a third-party principal, rather than to the market as a whole. As far as the market is concerned, a trade based on confidential information is no more "honest" because some third party may know of it so long as those on the other side of the trade remain in the dark.

7. The majority's statement, by arguing that market advantage is gained "through" deception, unfortunately seems to embrace an error in logic: Conflating causation and correlation. That the misappropriator may both deceive the source and "simultaneously" hurt the public no more shows a causal "connection" between the two than the fact that the sun both gives some people a tan and "simultaneously" nourishes plants demonstrates that melanin production in humans causes plants to grow. In this case, the only element common to the deception and the harm is that both are the result of the same antecedent cause—namely, using nonpublic information. But such use, even for securities trading, is not illegal, and the consequential deception of the source follows an entirely divergent branch of causation than does the harm to the public. The trader thus "gains his advantageous market position through" the use of nonpublic information, whether or not deception is involved; the deception has no effect on the existence or extent of his advantage.

II

I am also of the view that O'Hagan's conviction for violating Rule 14e-3(a) cannot stand.... According to the majority, prohibiting trading on nonpublic information is necessary to prevent such supposedly hard-to-prove fraudulent acts and practices as trading on information obtained from the buyer in breach of a fiduciary duty, and possibly "warehousing," whereby the buyer tips allies prior to announcing the tender offer and encourages them to purchase the target company's stock....

[E]ven further assuming that the Commission's misappropriation theory is a valid basis for direct liability, I fail to see how Rule 14e-3(a)'s elimination of the requirement of a breach of fiduciary duty is "reasonably designed" to prevent the underlying "fraudulent" acts. The majority's primary argument on this score is that in many cases " 'a breach of duty is likely but difficult to prove.'" Although the majority's hypothetical difficulties involved in a tipper-tippee situation might have some merit in the context of "classical" insider trading, there is no reason to suspect similar difficulties in "misappropriation" cases. In such cases, Rule 14e-3(a) requires the Commission to prove that the defendant "knows or has reason to know" that the nonpublic information upon which trading occurred came from the bidder or an agent of the bidder. Once the source of the information has been identified, it should be a simple task to obtain proof of any breach of duty. After all, it is the bidder itself that was defrauded in misappropriation cases, and there is no reason to suspect that the victim of the fraud would be reluctant to provide evidence against the perpetrator of the fraud.[12] There being no particular difficulties in proving a breach of duty

---

12. Even where the information is obtained from an agent of the bidder, and the tippee claims not to have known that the tipper violated a duty, there is still no justification for Rule 14e-3(a). First, in such circumstances the tipper himself would have violated his fiduciary duty and would be liable under the misappropriation theory, assuming that theory were valid. Facing such liability, there is no reason to suspect that the tipper would gratuitously protect the tippee. And if the tipper accurately testifies that the tippee was (falsely) told that the information was passed on without violating the tipper's own duties, one can question whether the tippee has in fact done anything illegal, even under the Commission's misappropriation theory. Given that the fraudulent breach of fiduciary duty would have been complete at the moment of the tip, the subsequent trading on that information by the tippee might well fail even the Commission's own construction of the "in connection with" requirement. Thus, even if the tipper might, in some circumstances, be inclined to protect the tippee, it is doubtful that the tippee would have violated the misappropriation theory in any event, and thus preventing such nonviolations cannot justify Rule 14e-3(a). Second, even were this scenario a legitimate concern, it would at most justify eliminating the requirement that the tippee "know" about the breach of duty. It would not explain Rule 14e-3(a)'s elimination of the requirement that there be such a breach.

in such circumstances, a rule removing the requirement of such a breach cannot be said to be "reasonably designed" to prevent underlying violations of the misappropriation theory. . . .

While enhancing the overall efficacy of the Williams Act may be a reasonable goal, it is not one that may be pursued through Section 14(e), which limits its grant of rulemaking authority to the prevention of fraud, deceit, and manipulation. As we have held in the context of Section 10(b), "not every instance of financial unfairness constitutes fraudulent activity." *Chiarella*, 445 U.S. at 232. Because, in the context of misappropriation cases, Rule 14e-3(a) is not a means "reasonably designed" to prevent persons from engaging in fraud "in connection with" a tender offer, it exceeds the Commission's authority under Section 14(e), and respondent's conviction for violation of that Rule cannot be sustained.

13

Shareholder Voting and Going Private Transactions

A. Management Solicitations

2. Shareholder Proposals

Page 833. At the end of the first full paragraph, insert the following:

In Exchange Act Release No. 40018, May 21, 1998, the Commission revised Rule 14-8 by formally overturning its *"Cracker Barrel"* position. As a result, employment-related shareholder proposals are now treated the same as any other proposals for purposes of applying the "ordinary business" exclusion. The Commission also made some other minor changes, recasting the instruction for the rule into a simpler "question and answer" format and amending Rule 14-4 to clarify its position on management's exercise of discretionary voting authority when management has been advised of shareholder proposal that is not included in its solicitation materials under Rule 14a-8.

In making these relatively discrete changes, the Commission chose not to adopt a number of more significant amendments that it had proposed in 1997. For example, it did not adopt the proposed mechanism that would have allowed a certain percentage of shareholders to override an "ordinary business" exclusion.

||14||
Corporate Takeovers

B. The Early Warning System: Section 13(d)

Page 875. At the end of note 5, add the following:

In early 1998, the SEC amended the Section 13(d)/(g) rules to do what it had contemplated in 1989. Exchange Act Rel. No. 39538, January 12, 1998. Now all passive investors owning less than 20 percent of the issuer's securities, not just institutional ones, can use the simplified reporting of Schedule 13G. When a noninstitutional investor increases or decreases its holdings by more than 5 percent, a *prompt* amendment is required.

C. Tender Offer Regulation: Controlling the Bidder

Page 881. Insert at the end of Section 1:

In conjunction with its "aircraft carrier" release described in Chapter 4, *supra*, the SEC also published a release proposing rules that would liberalize the communications and disclosure requirements in connection with merger and takeover transactions. Securities Act Rel. No. 7607, November 3, 1998. The Commission observed that when securities are offered as consideration in such a deal, the '33 Act comes into play, significantly limiting what participants can say and when they can say it. In addition, takeovers today are often accompanied by proxy solicitations, bringing that

■ | Page 881.

distinct set of rules into play. The proposals thus seek to rationalize the merger and acquisition process, creating a unitary set of rules governing disclosure and communications regardless of the terms of the transaction. Among the more significant proposals, according to the release, are the following:

- relax the current restrictions on communications with security holders to provide the market with more information on a timely basis; in particular:
  - permit free communications before the filing of a registration statement in connection with either a stock tender offer or a stock merger transaction;
  - permit free communications before the filing of a proxy statement (whether or not a takeover transaction is involved);
  - permit free communications about a planned tender offer without triggering the "commencement" of the offer, requiring the filing and dissemination of information;
- harmonize the various communications principles applicable to business combinations under the Securities Act, tender offer rules and proxy rules; in particular:
  - eliminate the confidential treatment now available for merger proxy statements;
- reduce the disparate treatment of stock and cash tender offers by permitting stock tender offers to commence upon the filing of a Securities Act registration statement;
- simplify the regulatory scheme by integrating the disclosure requirements for tender offers, going private transactions, and other extraordinary transactions into a new "1000" series of Regulation S-K, referred to as "Regulation M-A";
- combine the current schedules for issuer and third-party tender offers into a single schedule available for all tender offers, entitled "Schedule TO";
- require a "plain English" summary term sheet in all cash tender offers, cash mergers, and going private transactions;
- update the financial statement requirements for takeover transactions; in particular:
  - eliminate the need to file financial statements for target companies in most cash mergers to harmonize with the treatment of cash tender offers;
  - clarify when financial statements of the acquiring company are not required in cash mergers; and when financial statements are required, reduce the financial statements required for the acquiror from three to two years;

14. Corporate Takeovers   Page 881.

- clarify when the bidder's financial statements are not required in cash tender offers; and when financial statements are required in third-party offers, reduce the requirement from three years to two;
- require pro forma and related financial information in cash tender offers where the bidder intends to engage in a back-end stock merger;
- reduce the financial statements required for non-reporting target companies in stock mergers;
- permit a subsequent offering period, similar to that available in many United Kingdom tender offers, during which security holders can tender their shares for a limited period after completion of a tender offer;
- clarify the rule that requires issuers to report any intended repurchases of their securities after a third-party tender offer has commenced (Rule 13e-1), and require information to be disseminated on a timely basis; and
- clarify the rule that prohibits purchases outside a tender offer (Rule 10b-13), codify prior interpretations of and exemptions from the rule, and redesignate it as Rule 14e-5.

15
The Enforcement of the Securities Laws

C. More on the Private Enforcement of the Securities Laws

1. Champion of the Little Guy: The Class Action

Page 975. At the end of the last full paragraph, insert the following.

The Reform Act was just the first shoe to fall on the plaintiff counsel's aggressive pursuit of class actions. In 1998, Congress returned to the subject of securities class actions by enacting the Securities Litigation Uniform Standards Act, which amends Section 18 of the Securities Act to confer on the federal courts the exclusive jurisdiction over most securities class actions. The Uniform Standards Act reflects Congress's belief that an unintended consequence of the Reform Act was that the plaintiff's bar frequently avoided substantive and procedural standards imposed by the Reform Act to address abuses of the securities class action by filing their suits in state courts. *See* Painter, Responding to a False Alarm: Federal Preemption of State Securities Fraud Causes of Action, 84 Cornell L. Rev. 1 (1998). To counter such a migration to state courts, the Uniform Standard Act preempts state court jurisdiction for class action suits involving "covered securities," a term defined in Section 18(b) of the Securities Act that includes NYSE and Amex as well as NASDAQ National Market System securities. Class actions are defined as suits that seek relief on behalf of 50 or more persons. The Uniform Standards Act excludes several types of suits from its otherwise broad preemptive effects. The most notable of its exclusions is the so-called Delaware carve-out that preserves the state court's jurisdiction to hear certain state law fiduciary claims in which misreprsentation may be an issue; such suits primarily arise in connection with statements by officers or directors in connection with tender offers, mergers, and other transactions. By permitting such suits to continue to be brought in state court, the Uniform Standards Act preserves a rich and quickly developing body of state fiduciary duty law. *See generally* Hamermesh, Calling Off the Lynch Mob: The Corporate Director's Fiduciary Disclosure Duty, 49 Vand. L. Rev. 1087 (1996).

Page 977. Add the following new material after the carryover paragraph:

In *Epstein v. MCA, Inc.*, 126 F.3d 1235 (9th 1997), a divided Ninth Circuit panel held that the Delaware Supreme Court judgment in *Matsushita*, which affirmed the settlement of *both* the state fiduciary law and federal securities law claims, violated the Due Process Clause. The court reasoned that the absent plaintiffs who were pursuing their securities law claims in federal court were not adequately represented in the state court settlement. The majority emphasized that Delaware counsel suffered from a conflict of interest. Because the Delaware action's counsel could not represent the Exchange Act claims in state court, the Ninth Circuit viewed him as being in competition with the parallel class action in the federal court, reasoning that any success in the federal action would reduce the fees that Delaware counsel would receive. With respect to this conflict of interest the court observed:

> It was plainly in the best interest of counsel to settle the federal claims at any price. For them, any settlement was better than no settlement because settlement was the only way they could make any money on the federal claims—indeed, given that the state claims were essentially worthless, it was the only way that Delaware counsel could get any compensation at all.

The court therefore concluded adequate representation as demanded by due process of law was lacking.

5. Secondary Liability

a. *Aiding and Abetting*

Page 1019. Add the following after *Central Bank* and before the Notes and Questions.

Wright v. Ernst & Young LLP
152 F.3d 169 (2d Cir. 1998), cert. denied, 1999 U.S. Lexis 602 (1999)

OPINION OF MESKILL, CIRCUIT JUDGE. Plaintiff-appellant Irene Wright appeals from a final judgment rendered in the United States District Court for the Southern District of New York ... dismissing her amended class action complaint charging defendant accounting firm Ernst & Young LLP with making materially false representations in connection with BT Office Products sale of common stock, all in violation of § 10(b) of the Securities Exchange Act of 1934 ... and ... Rule 10b-5. ...

...

DISCUSSION

1. Actionable Statements and § 10(b)

Wright first argues that because a defendant can incur primary liability under the Act for false statements that are not directly communicated to the public, there is no requirement that the false statement be attributed to the defendant at the time of its dissemination. Thus, Wright maintains that although BT's press release attributes no statement to Ernst & Young, the amended complaint nevertheless alleges a false statement within the meaning of § 10(b) because it alleges that Ernst & Young "assured" BT of the accuracy of its 1995 financial results, knowing that BT would, in turn, promptly disseminate those results to investors in the press release.

Further, Wright argues that even if the amended complaint does not allege conduct amounting to a false statement, it does state a § 10(b) cause of action under post-Central Bank authority because Ernst & Young is alleged to have "substantially participated" in the fraud. *See SEC v. First Jersey Securities*, 101 F.3d 1450, 1471 (2d Cir. 1996) ("Primary liability may be imposed 'not only on persons who made fraudulent misrepresentations but also on those who had knowledge of the fraud and assisted in its perpetration.'" ...

We conclude that Wright's arguments are foreclosed by *Central Bank* and by our recent decision in *Shapiro v. Cantor*, 123 F.3d 717 (2d Cir. 1997). ...

Prior to the Supreme Court's decision in *Central Bank*, a number of federal courts held that the strictures of § 10(b) reached not only those who actually make a material misstatement, but also those who aid and abet such a violation. *See Central Bank*, 511 U.S. at 169. ...

In *Central Bank*, the Supreme Court addressed the legitimacy of secondary liability claims in private actions brought pursuant to § 10(b). The Court concluded from the text of the Act that Congress never intended to impose secondary liability under § 10(b) and thus the Act "does not itself reach those who aid and abet . . . [but] prohibits only the making of a material misstatement (or omission) or the commission of a manipulative act." *Central Bank*, 511 U.S. at 177. The Court further observed that authorizing a § 10(b) cause of action based on aiding and abetting would circumvent the "reliance" requirement of Rule 10b-5 by allowing a plaintiff to prevail "without any showing that the plaintiff relied upon the aider and abettor's statements or actions." Id. at 180; *see also Basic v. Levinson*, 485 U.S. 224, 243 (1988) (rejecting liability under Rule 10b-5 without reliance). However, the Court did not hold that secondary actors are always free from liability under the Act. Rather, secondary actors like accountants may be held liable as primary violators if all the requirements for primary liability are met, including "a material misstatement (or omission) on which a purchaser or seller of securities relies." *Central Bank*, 511 U.S. at 191.

In the wake of *Central Bank*, federal courts have differed over the threshold required for a secondary actor's conduct to implicate primary liability. As Judge Gleeson of the Eastern District of New York observed,

> [S]ome courts have held that a third party's review and approval of documents containing fraudulent statements is not actionable under Section 10(b) because one must make the material misstatement or omission in order to be a primary violator. *See, e.g., In re Kendall Square Research Corporation Securities Litigation*, 868 F. Supp. 26, 28 (D. Mass. 1994) (accountant's "review and approval" of financial statements and prospectuses insufficient); *Vosgerichian v. Commodore International*, 862 F. Supp. 1371, 1378 (E.D. Pa. 1994) (allegations that accountant "advised" and "guid[ed]" client in making allegedly fraudulent misrepresentations insufficient).

Other [courts] have held that third parties may be primarily liable for statements made by others in which the defendant had significant participation. *See, e.g., In re Software Toolworks*, 50 F.3d 615, 628 n.3 (9th Cir. 1994) (accountant may be primarily liable based on its "significant role in drafting and editing" a letter sent by the issuer to the SEC); . . . *In re ZZZZ Best Securities Litigation*, 864 F. Supp. 960, 970 (C.D. Cal. 1994) (an accounting firm that was "intricately involved" in the creation of false documents and their "resulting deception" is a primary violator of section 10(b)).

These two differing approaches have been characterized respectively as the "bright line" test and the "substantial[] participat[ion]" test. Id.; *see also Anixter v. Home-Stake Prod. Co.*, 77 F.3d 1215, 1226-27 (10th Cir. 1996).

■I 15. The Enforcement of the Securities Laws   Page 1019. I■

In *Shapiro*, we followed the "bright line" test after observing that "'[i]f *Central Bank* is to have any real meaning, a defendant must actually make a false or misleading statement in order to be held liable under Section 10(b). Anything short of such conduct is merely aiding and abetting, and no matter how substantial that aid may be, it is not enough to trigger liability under Section 10(b).'" *Shapiro*, 123 F.3d at 720.... We also observed that because § 10(b) and Rule 10b-5 focus on fraud made in connection with the sale or purchase of securities, a defendant must "'know or should know'" that his representation would be communicated to investors. Id. at 720 (quoting *Anixter*, 77 F.3d at 1226). "There is no requirement that the alleged violator directly communicate misrepresentations to [investors] for primary liability to attach." *Anixter*, 77 F.3d at 1226. However, contrary to Wright's argument, a secondary actor cannot incur primary liability under the Act for a statement not attributed to that actor at the time of its dissemination. Such a holding would circumvent the reliance requirements of the Act, as "[r]eliance only on representations made by others cannot itself form the basis of liability." Id. at 1225. Thus, the misrepresentation must be attributed to that specific actor at the time of public dissemination, that is, in advance of the investment decision. *See In re Kendall Square Research Corp. Sec. Litigation*, 868 F. Supp. at 28 (where accountant did not issue a report on the company's financial statements, but merely "reviewed and approved" them, the accountant could not be liable for a material misstatement)....

In this case, BT's press release did not attribute any assurances to Ernst & Young and, in fact, did not mention Ernst & Young at all. Thus, Ernst & Young neither directly nor indirectly communicated misrepresentations to investors. Therefore, the amended complaint failed to allege that Ernst & Young made "a material misstatement (or omission) on which a purchaser or seller of securities relie[d]." *Central Bank*, 511 U.S. at 191. Moreover, as the district court aptly recognized, because the press release contained a clear and express warning that no audit had yet been completed, there is no basis for Wright to claim that Ernst & Young had endorsed the accuracy of those results. We therefore agree with the district court that holding Ernst & Young primarily liable under the Act "in spite of its clearly tangential role in the alleged fraud would effectively revive aiding and abetting liability under a different name, and would therefore run afoul of the Supreme Court's holding in *Central Bank*." Wright, 1997 WL 563782, at *3.

Wright also argues that under the post-Central Bank authority of this Circuit, the amended complaint nevertheless states a cause of action because Ernst & Young is alleged to have "substantially participated" in the fraud. Specifically, Wright cites our decision in *First Jersey*, 101 F.3d at 1471, for the proposition that "[p]rimary liability may be imposed 'not only on persons who made fraudulent misrepresentations but also on those who

71

had knowledge of the fraud and assisted in its perpetration.'"... Wright's argument is unpersuasive.

In *First Jersey*, we affirmed the imposition of primary liability under § 10(b) on Robert Brennan, the president, chief executive and sole owner of First Jersey Securities, Inc. Brennan had directed his employees to make false and misleading statements to customers. We held Brennan liable for securities fraud in his capacity as a "controlling person," that is, for fraud planned and directed by upper level management. Id. at 1471-74. Here, we confront alleged fraud by accountants—secondary actors who may no longer be held primarily liable under § 10(b) for mere knowledge and assistance in the fraud....

In 1995, Congress authorized the SEC to bring enforcement actions against those who "knowingly provide[] substantial assistance to another person" in violation of the federal securities laws. *See* Private Securities Litigation Reform Act of 1995, Pub. L. No. 104-67, § 104, 109 Stat. 737, 757, codified in 15 U.S.C. § 78t(f). That congressional act did not create a private cause of action.

Finally, Wright argues that we should follow other jurisdictions that have adopted the substantial participation test. *See In re Software Toolworks Inc. Sec. Litigation*, 50 F.3d at 628 n.3; *In re ZZZZ Best Sec. Litigation*, 864 F. Supp. at 970 n.12. We decline to do so. *See Shapiro*, 123 F.3d at 720. Moreover, even under the "substantial participation" test, we would be hard pressed to conclude that the amended complaint alleged an actionable misrepresentation within the meaning of §10(b). *See Cashman v. Coopers & Lybrand*, 877 F. Supp. 425, 432 (N.D. Ill. 1995) (where court applies substantial participation test, accounting firm may not incur primary liability for a misstatement unless that statement is "certified, audited, prepared or reported"); *see also Robin v. Arthur Young & Co.*, 915 F.2d 1120, 1125 (7th Cir. 1990) (accounting firm could not be held liable for aiding and abetting under pre-*Central Bank* standard even where company alleged that "but for" accounting firm's consent, company would not have issued prospectus containing false and misleading financial statements), *cert. denied*, 499 US. 923 (1991)....

CONCLUSION

Central Bank of Denver v. First Interstate Bank of Denver, 511 U.S. 164 (1994), and *Shapiro v. Cantor*, 123 F.3d 717 (2d Cir. 1997), foreclose primary liability under the Act for false or misleading statements made by Ernst & Young because no false or misleading statement was attributed to Ernst & Young at the time of public dissemination. Accordingly, the district court did not err in dismissing the amended complaint on that ground....

D. The Duties of the Securities Lawyer

Page 1057. Add the following new material after the paragraph immediately before the Problems.

3. The Attorney as Aider and Abettor. An interesting application of the aiding and abetting standard to an attorney is *S.E.C. v. Fehn*, 97 F.3d 738 (9th Cir. 1996), *cert. denied*, 118 S. Ct. 59 (1997). Fehn, an attorney, was retained by CTI Technical, Inc. when the SEC commenced its investigation of CTI's IPO. Fehn learned that CTI had not filed the Form 10-Q quarterly reports, as required by Section 15(d) of the Exchange Act, after making its IPO. Fehn also was aware that CTI had failed to disclose in its registration statement that Edwin "Bud" Wheeler was the company's promoter and controlled its nominal directors. Fehn advised Wheeler that CTI was required to file the quarterly Form 10-Q and discussed with him the need to disclose Wheeler's role in the corporation. Wheeler flatly refused to make the disclosure; Fehn later testified that he told Wheeler it was his professional opinion that such disclosures were unnecessary and that it would likely compromise Wheeler's ability to assert his Fifth Amendment privilege if CTI made full disclosure of Wheeler's status. An employee of CTI prepared a draft Form 10-Q that stated Wheeler had just recently been appointed CEO and president. It did not disclose that he promoted, incorporated, and controlled CTI. Fehn reviewed and edited the draft Form 10-Q but did not alter its disclosure misrepresenting Wheeler's status.

The court held CTI's quarterly report violated Rule 10b-5, not only because it misrepresented Wheeler's position but also because it failed to disclose CTI's contingent liability to purchasers in the IPO who could recover because the registration statement was materially misleading in failing to disclose Wheeler's relationship to CTI. The Ninth Circuit held that Fehn's review and editing of the Form 10-Q constituted substantial assistance in CTI's securities violations. The Ninth Circuit rejected Fehn's argument that he fell within the "good faith and reasonable efforts" defense of *In re Carter and Johnson*; the court reasoned instead that the defense was not available since the SEC's disclosure requirements clearly required disclosure of the items Fehn concurred could be either omitted or misrepresented.

It is worth noting the following policy consideration the court invoked to support upholding a permanent injunction against Fehn:

> We observe, furthermore, that effective regulation of the issuance and trading of securities depends, fundamentally, on securities lawyers such as

Fehn properly advising their clients of the disclosure requirements and other relevant provisions of the securities regulations. Securities regulation in this country is premised on open disclosure, and it is therefore incumbent upon practitioners like Fehn to be highly familiar with the disclosure requirements and to insist that their clients comply with them.

Id. at 1294.

What would result if Fehn were a labor lawyer who had been retained by CTI because of a formal investigation by the Equal Employment Opportunity Commission for alleged discriminatory promotion practices? Assume in that position that he approved and edited a Form 10-Q that did not disclose (nor did its earlier registration statement) that CTI had unlawfully discriminated against women and minorities such that it potentially was liable for substantial damages its discriminatory practices had caused present and former employees. Would the result be the same?

E. The SEC's Power to Discipline Professionals

Page 1062. Add the following at the end of the carryover paragraph.

In response to an unqualified rebuke in *Checkosy v. SEC*, 139 F.3d 221 (D.C. Cir. 1998), that Rule 102(e) was too vague with respect to its "improper professional conduct" standard, the Commission amended its disciplinary rule. Securities Act Release No. 7593 (Oct. 19, 1998). The amendment adds the following:

> 102(e)(1) . . . (iv) With respect to persons licensed to practice as accountants, "improper professional conduct" . . . means:
> (A) Intentional or knowing conduct, including reckless conduct, that results in a violation of applicable professional standards; or
> (B) Either of the following two types of negligent conduct:
> (1) A single instance of highly unreasonable conduct that results in a violation of applicable professional standards in circumstances in which an accountant knows, or should know, that heightened scrutiny is warranted.
> (2) Repeated instances of unreasonable conduct, each resulting in a violation of applicable professional standards, that indicate a lack of competence to practice before the Commission.

■I 15. The Enforcement of the Securities Laws   Page 1062. I■

To what extent does the above amendment address *Checkosky's* condemnation that Rule 102(e)(1)(ii) "yields no clear and coherent standard for violations . . . "? For a close review of experiences under Rule 102(e) prior to its recent amendment, *see* Report of the Task Force on Rule 102(e) Proceedings: Rule 102(e) Sanctions Against Accountants, 52 Bus. Law 965 (1997).

16
Regulation of the Securities Markets and Securities Professionals

A. *The Structure of Regulation and the Evolution of the Securities Markets*

Page 1079. Add the following after the carryover paragraph:

Exchange Act Rel. No. 38672
May 23, 1997

Stock markets play a critical role in the economic life of the United States. The phenomenal growth of the U.S. markets over the past 60 years is a direct result of investor confidence in those markets. Technological trends over the past two decades have also contributed greatly to this success. In particular, technology has provided a vastly greater number of investment and execution choices, increased market efficiency, and reduced trading costs. These developments have enhanced the ability of U.S. exchanges to implement efficient market linkages and advanced the goals of the national market system ("NMS").

At the same time, however, technological changes have posed significant challenges for the existing regulatory framework, which is ill-equipped to respond to innovations in U.S. and cross-border trading. Specifically, two key developments highlight the need for a more forward-looking, flexible regulatory framework: (1) the exponential growth of trading systems that present comparable alternatives to traditional exchange trading; and (2) the development of automated mechanisms that facilitate access to foreign markets from the United States. The Commission estimates that alternative trading systems currently handle almost 20 percent of the orders in over-the-counter ("OTC") stocks and almost 4 percent of orders in securities listed on the New York Stock Exchange ("NYSE"). The explosive growth of alternative trading systems over the past several years has significant implications for public secondary market regulation. Even though many of these systems provide essentially the same services as traditional markets, most alternative trading systems are regulated as broker-dealers. As a result, they have been subject to regulations designed primarily to address traditional brokerage, rather than market, activities. For example, these systems are typically subject to oversight by self-regulatory organizations ("SROs") that themselves operate exchanges or quotation systems, which raises inherent competitive concerns.

At the same time, alternative trading systems are not fully integrated into the national market system. As a result, activity on alternative trading systems is not fully disclosed to, or accessible by, public investors. The trading activity on these systems may not be adequately surveilled for market manipulation and fraud. Moreover, these trading systems have no obligation to provide investors a fair opportunity to participate in their systems or to treat their participants fairly, nor do they have an obligation to ensure that they have sufficient capacity to handle trading demand. These concerns together with the increasingly important role of alternative trading systems, call into question the fairness of current regulatory requirements, the effectiveness of existing NMS mechanisms, and the quality of public secondary markets. . . .

II. REGULATION OF DOMESTIC MARKETS

A. TECHNOLOGICAL ADVANCES

Securities markets serve several basic functions that are critical to facilitating investment and, as a result, materially influence the long-term financial security of a large segment of the population. For example, markets provide the forum for individuals to invest in securities and for financial instruments to be readily converted into cash when needed. Securities markets also serve as a fundamental indicator of national and international economic health, in part because they reveal investors' judgments about the potential earning capacity of corporations. They help to raise and efficiently allocate capital by providing a reliable means of valuing assets and facilitating the flow of capital into private enterprise. They also allocate capital toward productive uses by providing a forum where stocks can compete for investment dollars. U.S. securities markets have been highly successful at fulfilling these functions and are consistently the world's largest, most liquid, efficient, and fair. Moreover, U.S. markets have continued to attract foreign listings and investors even as other markets become more competitive. This success has come about, in part, because the strength and stability of U.S. markets have allowed people throughout the world to feel confident investing a large percentage of their personal wealth in the future of companies trading on those markets.

The ability of U.S. markets to use technology to increase efficiency, reduce the costs of trading, and respond to changing investor demands has also contributed significantly to the success of our markets. Over the past three decades, technology has transformed U.S. markets. Investors, particularly the growing institutional investor base, now have numerous alternatives to traditional exchange trading and the OTC market. Similarly, market participants (including broker-dealers, issuers, and service providers) have integrated technological advancements into their trading and marketing activities. For example, some broker-dealers have made communications with retail customers more efficient by offering various services through the Internet.

As technology has broadened the services that can be delivered by both markets and market intermediaries, market services have become unbundled from traditional brokerage or exchange services. While some entities that perform brokerage services have also begun to perform some of the traditional functions of a stock exchange, other entities (including information vendors, service bureaus, and routing services) now provide many of the services historically provided by exchanges and broker-dealers. One significant example of this has been the development and growing popularity of alternative trading systems, such as the Real-Time Trading Service operated by Instinet Corporation ("Instinet"), The Island System ("Island"), Portfolio System for Institutional Trading ("POSIT"), and the Arizona Stock Exchange ("AZX"), which allow institutions and other market participants to electronically execute trades in a variety of ways. These and other alternative trading systems have grown to account for a significant percentage of the trading volume of the U.S. securities markets, particularly within the last five years. In 1994, the Commission's Division of Market Regulation reported that alternative trading systems accounted for 13 percent of the volume in Nasdaq securities and 1.4 percent of the trading volume in NYSE-listed securities. In comparison, the Commission estimates that alternative trading systems currently handle almost 20 percent of the orders in Nasdaq securities and almost 4 percent of orders in NYSE-listed stocks.

Technology has also significantly altered the operation of exchange and OTC markets. For example, most exchanges have designed systems that allow members to route orders electronically to the exchange for execution. The NYSE has also established after-hours crossing systems that automate the execution of single stock orders and baskets of securities, and the Cincinnati Stock Exchange ("CSE") is now a fully automated exchange where members effect transactions through computers located in their own offices. Dealer markets have been similarly transformed. Dealer markets traditionally consisted of loosely organized groups of individual dealers that traded securities OTC, without formal consolidation of orders or trading. As individual dealers and associations of dealers have employed technology to make OTC markets more efficient, however, dealer markets in certain instruments have become organized to such an extent that they have assumed many of the characteristics of exchange markets. This is particularly true in markets that trade instruments that are also listed on registered exchanges. For example, the Nasdaq market, operated by the National Association of Securities Dealers, Inc. ("NASD"), consolidates trading interest of multiple dealers on a computer screen that is displayed in real-time to its members and provides a mechanism for dealers to update displayed quotations. Additional services, such as SelectNet, allow dealers in the Nasdaq market to trade electronically. Through this technology, the NASD has been able to coordinate the dealer market more efficiently.

Overall, these developments have benefited investors by increasing efficiency and competition, reducing costs, and spurring further technological advancement of the entire market. In particular, for those market participants that have access to alternative trading systems, these systems have provided opportunities for the direct execution of orders without the active participation of an intermediary. Alternative markets are likely to grow as technology continues to drive the evolution of the equity markets.

B. Market Regulation

Whether trading electronically or through human intervention, investors are more likely to trade on a market when prices are current and reflect the value of securities, when they are confident that they will be able to buy and sell securities easily and inexpensively, and when they believe that they can trade on a market without being defrauded or without other investors having an unfair advantage. The competition for global investment capital among the world's exchanges and the many opportunities available to U.S. and foreign investors make it more important than ever for U.S. exchanges to protect these investor interests in order to attract order flow. Appropriate regulation is often necessary to protect these interests, by helping to ensure fair and orderly markets, to prevent fraud and manipulation, and to promote market coordination and competition for the benefit of all investors.

In the United States, Congress decided that these goals should be achieved primarily through the regulation of exchanges and through authority it granted to the Commission in 1975 ("1975 Amendments") to adopt rules that promote (1) economically efficient execution of securities transactions, (2) fair competition, (3) transparency, (4) investor access to the best markets, and (5) the opportunity for investors' orders to be executed without the participation of a dealer. In promulgating the Exchange Act, Congress gave the Commission means to achieve these and other goals of regulation, by requiring every market that meets the definition of exchange under the Exchange Act to either register as a national securities exchange or be exempted from registration on the basis of limited transaction volume. Congress also gave the exchanges authority to enforce their members' compliance with the goals of the securities laws and, in 1983, required every broker-dealer to become a member of an exchange or securities association. As SROs, every registered exchange and securities association is required to assist the Commission in assuring fair and honest markets, to have effective mechanisms for enforcing the goals of regulation, and to submit their rules for Commission review. This statutory structure has given the Commission ample authority to oversee securities markets and ensure compliance with the Exchange Act. Although regulation cannot prevent all manipulation, fraud, or collusion, it has proven effective in ridding markets of the most egregious of these practices and consequently in inspiring a high degree of investor confidence.

As a result of the technologically-driven developments discussed above, however, the distinctions among market service providers have become blurred, making it more difficult to determine whether any particular entity operates as an exchange, OTC market, broker, or dealer. For example, alternative trading systems incorporate features of both traditional markets and broker-dealers. Like traditional exchanges, alternative trading systems centralize orders and give participants control over the interaction of their orders. Like traditional broker-dealers, alternative trading systems are proprietary and, in some cases, maintain trading desks that facilitate participant trading. Because the activities of alternative trading systems include both traditional exchange and broker-dealer functions, it is often unclear whether such systems should register as exchanges, broker-dealers, or both. Under the existing statutory structure enacted by Congress, however, exchanges and broker-dealers are subject to significantly different obligations and responsibilities.

To date, the Commission has regulated many alternative markets as broker-dealers, rather than as exchanges, in order to foster the development of innovative trading mechanisms within the existing statutory framework. The determination as to whether any particular alternative trading system should be regulated as an exchange or broker-dealer has been decided on a case-by-case basis. This regulatory approach has had two significant, unintended effects: (1) it has subjected alternative trading systems to a regulatory scheme that is not particularly suited to their market activities; and (2) it has impeded effective integration, surveillance, enforcement, and regulation of the U.S. markets as a whole.

■ | Page 1079.   16. Regulation of the Securities Markets/Professionals | ■

1. The Current Regulatory Approach Applies Inappropriate Regulation to Alternative Trading Systems

As broker-dealers, alternative trading systems are subject to regulation designed primarily to address traditional brokerage activities rather than market activities. For example, broker-dealers are required to become members of the Securities Investor Protection Corporation ("SIPC"). While this membership is designed to protect customer funds and securities held by brokers, few alternative trading systems hold customer funds or securities. In addition, broker-dealers are required to be members of an SRO. Thus, alternative trading systems are subject to oversight by exchanges and the NASD, which operate their own markets. Because these markets often compete with alternative trading systems for order flow, there is an inherent conflict between SROs competitive concern as markets and their regulatory obligations to oversee alternative trading systems.

Regulating alternative trading systems as traditional broker-dealers, therefore, requires compliance by these systems with obligations that, in many cases, are not pertinent to their principal activities. As discussed below, traditional broker-dealer regulation also fails to address concerns raised by alternative trading systems' market activities.

2. The Current Regulatory Approach Impedes Effective Regulation

The Commission has repeatedly evaluated whether the case-by-case no-action approach has permitted adequate Commission oversight of secondary trading markets, particularly in light of the growth and evolving market significance of such systems. Prior to 1993, the low volume and relatively small number of alternative trading systems appeared to justify such an approach. In 1993, for example, in an attempt to evaluate the effects of regulating alternative trading systems as broker-dealers, the Commission's Division of Market Regulation conducted a study of the U.S. equity markets. This study concluded that, at that time, the Commission did not have sufficient regular information to evaluate the effects of alternative trading systems on the U.S. securities markets. Therefore, the Division of Market Regulation recommended that the Commission closely monitor the impact of the proliferation of such systems. In response to this recommendation, the Commission adopted a recordkeeping and reporting rule, Rule 17a-23, specifically for broker-dealers that operate alternative trading systems.

Because traditional broker-dealer regulation is not designed to apply to markets such as alternative trading systems, gaps have developed in the structures designed to ensure marketwide fairness, transparency, integrity, and stability. As discussed in greater detail below, the regulation of the most significant alternative trading systems under traditional broker-dealer regulation calls into question the accuracy of public quotation and trade information, and the fairness of the public secondary markets. In addition, such regulation may impair the detection and elimination of fraudulent and manipulative trading, and the mechanisms to ensure fair and equitable oversight and competition among markets.

a. Market Access and Fairness

While institutional investors are now the dominant players in U.S. financial markets, the United States still has the highest percentage of direct individual participation in the stock markets. Because the needs and interests of small individual investors, money managers, wealthy speculators, and large pension plans are not always the same, market regulation is intended to ensure that these diverse investors are treated fairly and have fair access to investment opportunities.

Specifically, the Exchange Act requires registered exchanges and securities associations to consider the public interest in administering their markets, to allocate reasonable fees equitably, and to establish rules designed to admit members fairly. While these provisions are based on the principle that qualified market participants should have fair access to the nation's securities markets, they are not intended to limit exchanges from having reasonable standards for access. Rather, fair access requirements are intended to prohibit unreasonably discriminatory denials of access. A denial of access would be reasonable, for example, if it were based on unbiased standards, such as capital and credit requirements, and if these standards were applied fairly.

The Exchange Act also requires registered exchanges and securities associations to establish rules that assure fair representation of members and investors in selecting directors and administering their organizations. The purpose of this requirement is to protect the rights and interests of the diverse members of registered exchanges and securities associations. In addition, because registered exchanges and securities associations are also SROs, they exercise governmental powers, such as the imposition of disciplinary sanctions on their members. Fair representation on the body responsible for disciplining members is, therefore, critical to the impartial enforcement of SRO rules.

Market regulation is also designed to remove barriers to fair competition, by prohibiting the rules of registered exchanges and securities associations from being anticompetitive, and by providing for Commission review of the rules of registered exchanges and securities associations. To further emphasize the goal of vigorous competition, Congress required the Commission to consider the competitive effects of exchange rules, as well as the Commission's own rules.

■❙ Page 1079.   16. Regulation of the Securities Markets/Professionals ❙■

The Commission's authority to review the actions of registered exchanges and securities associations has prevented the implementation of numerous rules that would have been anticompetitive or otherwise detrimental to the market. For example, in December 1990, the American Stock Exchange ("Amex") submitted a rule proposal to the Commission that would have excluded the orders of competing dealers (*i.e.*, regional exchange specialists and third market makers) from its order routing system and would have imposed trading restrictions on competing dealers in Amex securities. Because the exclusions and restrictions applied only to competing dealers and not to other off-floor broker-dealers trading for their own accounts, the proposal raised market access and competitive concerns. After receiving numerous negative public comments regarding the Amex's proposal, the Commission staff recommended that the Amex either amend or withdraw the proposal. Similarly, several exchanges have proposed prohibiting customer orders from being executed through the exchanges' automated systems for guaranteed execution of small customer orders, if those customers used computer and communications technology to generate and transmit those orders. Such a proposal, if implemented, would have had the effect of discouraging the use of new, innovative technology. The tendency to try to discourage innovation in order to protect existing practices is not new. In 1987, for example, the Commission set aside the NYSE's denial of the requests of two of its members for permission to install telephone connections on the floor to enable the members to communicate with their customers.

The fair access and treatment requirements in the Exchange Act are intended to ensure that exchanges and securities associations operating markets treat investors and their participants fairly. Under the current regulatory approach, however, there is no regulatory redress for unfair denials or limitations of access by alternative trading systems, or for unreasonably discriminatory actions taken against, or retaliatory fees imposed upon, participants in these systems. The availability of redress for such discriminatory actions may not be critical when alternative trading systems disclose any discriminatory practices to their participants and when market participants are able to substitute the services of one alternative trading system with those of another. However, when an alternative trading system has no other serious competitor, such as when it has a significantly large percentage of the volume of trading, discriminatory actions may be anticompetitive because market participants must use such trading system to remain competitive. Similarly, significant changes in the operations of alternative trading systems are not subject to either Commission or SRO review—even those changes that may be anticompetitive, unfair to a particular group of market participants, or that have significant effects on the primary public markets.

b. Market Transparency and Coordination

Securities markets have become increasingly interdependent because of the opportunities technology provides to link products, implement complex hedging strategies across markets, and trade on multiple markets simultaneously. While these opportunities benefit many investors, they can also create misallocations of capital, widespread inefficiency, and trading fragmentation if markets do not coordinate. Moreover, a lack of coordination among markets can increase system-wide risks. Congress adopted the 1975 Amendments, in part, to address these potential negative effects of a proliferation of markets. In the 1975 Amendments, Congress specifically endorsed the development of a national market system, and sought to clarify and strengthen the Commission's authority to promote the achievement of such a system. Because of uncertainty as to how technological and economic changes would affect the securities markets, Congress explicitly rejected mandating specific components of a national market system. Instead, Congress granted the Commission "maximum flexibility in working out the specific details" and "broad discretionary powers" to implement the development of a national market system in accordance with the goals of the 1975 Amendments. The SROs and the Commission have worked hard to achieve these goals.

Recent evidence suggests that the failure of the current regulatory approach to fully coordinate trading on alternative trading systems into national market systems mechanisms has impaired the quality and pricing efficiency of secondary equity markets, particularly in light of the explosive growth in trading volume on such alternative trading systems. Although these systems are available to some institutions, orders on these systems frequently are not available to the general investing public. The ability of market makers and specialists to display different and potentially superior prices on these alternative trading systems than those displayed to the general public created, in the past, the potential for a two-tiered market.

For example, during the Commission's recent investigation of Nasdaq trading, analyses of trading in the two most significant trading systems for Nasdaq securities (Instinet and SelectNet) revealed that the majority of bids and offers displayed by market makers in these systems were better than those posted publicly on Nasdaq. Moreover, the Commission found that, because they could trade with other market professionals through non-public alternative trading systems, market makers did not have a sufficient economic incentive to adjust their public quotations to reflect more competitive prices. Ultimately, the wider spreads quoted publicly by market makers increased the transaction costs paid by public customers, impaired the ability of some institutional investors to obtain favorable prices in those securities, and placed institutions at a potential disadvantage in price negotiations.

In response to these findings, the Commission recently took steps to bring greater transparency into the trading environment of certain alternative trading systems. In September 1996, the Commission adopted rules that require a market maker or specialist to make publicly available any superior prices that it privately offers through certain types of alternative trading systems known as electronic communications networks or ECNs. The new rules permit an ECN to fulfill these obligations on behalf of market makers using its system, by submitting its best market maker bid/ask quotations to an SRO for inclusion into public quotation displays ("ECN Display Alternative").

These rules, however, were not intended to fully coordinate trading on alternative trading systems with public market trading. While these rules will help integrate orders on certain trading systems into the public quotation system, they only affect trading that is conducted by market makers and specialists; activity of other participants on alternative trading systems remains undisclosed to the public market unless the system voluntarily undertakes to disclose all of its best bid/ask prices. Moreover, whether an ECN reflects the best bid/ask quotations on behalf of market makers and specialists that participate in its system is wholly voluntary. Specifically, ECNs are under no obligation to integrate orders submitted into their systems into the public quotation system, and the central quotation system is not currently required to accept ECNs as participants.

Because a majority of trading interest on alternative trading systems is not integrated into the national market system, price transparency is impaired and dissemination of quotation information is incomplete. These developments are contrary to the goals the Commission enunciated over twenty years ago when it noted that an essential purpose of a national market system

> is to make information on prices, volume, and quotes for securities in all markets available to all investors, so that buyers and sellers of securities, wherever located, can make informed investment decisions and not pay more than the lowest price at which someone is willing to sell and not sell for less than the highest price a buyer is prepared to offer.

This development also thwarts congressional goals for a national market system, where the best trading opportunities are to be made accessible to all customers, not just those customers who, due to their size or sophistication, may avail themselves of prices in alternative trading systems not currently available in the public quotation system.

c. Market Surveillance

Market regulation critically enhances the Commission's ability to surveil market activity as a whole in order to prevent fraud and manipulation, which can jeopardize market integrity and stability. Exchanges and securities associations such as the NASD act as SROs and, as such, are responsible not only for complying with the Exchange Act, but also for carrying out the purposes of the Exchange Act, principally by enforcing member compliance with the provisions of the Exchange Act and the rules promulgated thereunder, as well as the exchanges' or associations' own rules. This requires exchanges and securities associations to establish rules and procedures to prevent fraud and manipulation and promote just and equitable principles of trade, typically by establishing audit trails, surveillance, and disciplinary programs. It also requires exchanges and securities associations to enforce the antifraud provisions of the federal securities laws. These requirements are essential to ensure that SROs implement the goals established by Congress vigilantly and effectively. In addition, exchanges and securities associations serve a critical regulatory function by establishing and enforcing just and equitable principles of trade, and by providing a mechanism for preventing inappropriate behavior that damages market integrity, even if such behavior does not rise to the level of fraud under the Exchange Act. As a result of these requirements, exchanges and securities associations carry out much of the day-to-day surveillance for, and initial investigation of, trading improprieties, rule violations, and fraud.

Although the broker-dealers that operate many of the alternative trading systems have certain obligations to individual customers, because these systems are not SROs, they do not have the same market-wide enforcement and surveillance obligations as registered exchanges and the NASD. Moreover, SROs' current programs to surveil their own markets for fraud, insider trading, and market manipulation do not extend to observing quote activity on alternative trading systems. Specifically, although trades executed through certain alternative trading systems are reported to the NASD by either broker-dealer participants in such systems or by the broker-dealer operating the market, the NASD may not receive a consolidated picture of trading activity on alternative trading systems. Because activity on alternative trading systems is only reported to an SRO after a trade has been executed, SROs cannot fully supervise SROs' members' activities on those systems. In addition, because alternative trading systems are often reported as the counterparty to all trades between institutions executed through their systems, SRO surveillance mechanisms may not be able to identify the true counterparties of those trades. As a result, fraudulent or manipulative activity that an institution is carrying on through an alternative trading system may be masked by the overall activities of the system's other participants, and go uninvestigated. As more institutions use alternative trading systems to trade with each other, rather than with intermediaries, this could result in significant volume that is not integrated into SRO surveillance operations. Finally, alternative trading systems that compete with systems operated by SROs have repeatedly questioned whether particular SRO actions were driven by competitive, rather than regulatory motives. Thus, adequate oversight of alternative trading systems by SROs may be hindered by competitive concerns.

d. Market Stability and Systemic Risks

SROs have substantial, ongoing commitments to maintain sufficient system capacity, integrity, and security. The Commission has instituted a program to monitor capacity planning at SROs, so that it can take preemptive action if necessary, and meets with the SROs on a regular basis and reviews various aspects of their computer operations. In contrast, the Division of Market Regulation's experience in administering the Order Handling Rules and other broker-dealer rules has revealed that, in many cases, ECNs and other alternative trading systems may have serious capacity problems. Even though they have significant trading volume, under the current regulatory scheme ECNs and other alternative trading systems are not required to have sufficient computer capacity to meet ongoing trading demand or to withstand periods of extreme market volatility or other short-term surges in trading volume. Failure to integrate alternative trading systems into the Commission's programs to review and enhance the capacity of alternative trading systems jeopardizes efforts to ensure that all trade execution centers will remain operational during periods of market stress.

C. Conclusion

In sum, the current regulation of alternative trading systems does not address the market activities performed by such systems. As a result, such regulation may not have effectively met the congressional goals of protecting market participants from fraud and manipulation, promoting market coordination and stability, and ensuring regulatory fairness and fair competition.

NOTE

In Exchange Act Release No. 34-40760, December 8, 1998, the Commission took action. It broadened the definition of "exchange" in Rule 3b-16 to include, with certain exclusions, organizations that "bring together" orders of multiple buyers and sellers and that use established nondiscretionary methods for matching and executing these orders. This presumptively brings into the regulatory umbrella most significant alternative trading mechanisms. However, using its exemptive authority, the Commission then provided in new Regulation ATS that most "non-dominant" systems could

■| 16. Regulation of the Securities Markets/Professionals   Page 1105. |■

opt out of exchange regulation in favor of special broker-dealer regulation. A system that trades more than 5 percent of the volume of any national market system security to establish a link to a registered market in order to create a degree of transparency to the order routing process. Those with 20 percent or more of the trading volume in any such security would be subject to additional regulation, such as a requirement of nondiscrimination in access and ensuring that they build into their systems mechanisms for guaranteeing adequate systems capacity, integrity, and contingency planning.

Where does the customer stand in all this? In *Newton v. Merrill, Lynch, Pierce, Fenner & Smith*, 135 F.3d 267 (3d Cir. 1998) (en banc), the Third Circuit considered the question of whether the defendant broker-dealers defrauded their customers during a 1992-94 class period when they executed their orders at the readily available "national best bid and offer" price (NBBO)—the prevailing best published quote from among competing marketmakers—rather than engage in additional search efforts to find a better price, such as using the Instinet system. Plaintiffs argued that new technological developments had made such searches practicable, and that the duty of best execution is always an evolving one. Noting the SEC's recent revisions in this area, the court held that a reasonable trier of fact could infer that a deliberate failure to seek out a superior price *could* be a deceptive practice, and remanded for further proceedings on both the viability of the alternative search systems and whether the defendants acted with scienter.

As much as anything, *Newton* is interesting for its description of the broker's agency law based obligations to its customers. According to the court, "[s]ince it is understood by all that the client-principal seeks his own economic gain and the purpose of the agency is to help the client-principal achieve that objective, the broker-dealer, absent instruction to the contrary, is expected to use reasonable efforts to maximize the economic benefit to the client in the transaction." Id. at 270. That means "the best reasonably available price." Id. Though conceding that there is no bright-line definition of that term, the court concluded that it "is not so vague as to be without ascertainable content in the context of a particular trade or trades." Id. at 270-271. Hence, further factual inquiry with respect to plaintiffs' allegations was both necessary and appropriate.

C. *The Responsibilities of Brokers to their Customers*

3. **Suitability**

Page 1105.   Add the following at the end of the *Brown* case:

89

Banca Cremi, S.A. v. Alex. Brown & Sons, Inc.
132 F.3d 1017 (4th Cir. 1997)

[Banca Cremi, a Mexican bank with nearly $5 billion in assets, bought a number of collaterized mortgage obligations (CMOs) from the Baltimore-based investment banking firm of Alex. Brown & Co. CMOs are interests in pools of mortgage obligations. As commonly structured, the interests in a pool of mortgage obligations are divided into different "tranches"— classes which have different classes of risks and returns. Banca Cremi had purchased both "inverse floaters" and "inverse interest-only strips," both of which were at the high end of the risk spectrum. Inverse floaters have a fixed principal amount and earn interest at a rate that moves inversely to a specified index rate. They earn high returns if rates decline or remain constant, but lose substantial value if interest rates increase. Inverse IOs do not receive principal payments, but receive a rate of interest that also floats inversely to an index rate. At first, the bank played the CMO market aggressively, and made considerable profits. When interest rates went up unexpectedly in 1994, however, much of the CMO market collapsed and the bank lost around $21 million on an original purchase price of some $40 million.

Banca Cremi sued Alex. Brown on a number of grounds related to fraud and suitability. In general, it alleged a series of misrepresentations and nondisclosures relating to the risks associated with the kinds of CMO interests it had purchased. In considering defendants' motion for summary judgment, the court acknowledged, citing the *Brown* case, that the crucial issue in litigation like this under Rule 10b-5 is whether the plaintiff had a right to rely, and agreed that the proper standard for barring plaintiffs' claim is whether its failure of diligence amounted to recklessness. In discussing this issue, drawing from a list of factors as set forth in *Myers v. Finkle*, 950 F.2d 165 (4th Cir. 1991), Judge Magill said:]

> The first *Myers* factor, the sophistication of the investor, has long been a critical element in determining whether an investor was entitled to § 10(b) relief. See *Kohler v. Kohler Co.*, 319 F.2d 634, 642 (7th Cir. 1963) (considering an investor's "business acumen" and access to "extrinsic sources of sound business advice" to conclude there was no reliance, although the transaction might not have been fair if the investor had been a novice"); *List v. Fashion Park, Inc.*, 340 F.2d 457, 463-64 (2d Cir. 1965) (no reliance where investor was "an experienced and successful investor in securities" who did not ask his broker for information regarding the claimed omission). A sophisticated investor requires less information to call a "[mis-]representation into question" than would an unsophisticated investor. *Angelos*, 762 F.2d at 530. Likewise, when material information is omitted, a sophisticated investor is more

likely to "know [ ] enough so that the . . . omission still leaves him cognizant of the risk. *Id.*

When an investor is an individual, this Court looks to several factors to determine if the investor is sophisticated, including "wealth[,] . . . age, education, professional status, investment experience, and business background." *Myers,* 950 F.2d at 168. Some of these factors may not be perfectly suited for application to an institutional investor. *Cf.* C. Edward Fletcher, Sophisticated Investors Under the Federal Securities Laws, 1988 Duke L.J. 1081, 1149-53 (reviewing factors gauging sophistication of individual investors, and concluding that there should be a "conclusive presumption" that all institutional investors are sophisticated). However, the factors which are relevant to an institution strongly support the sophistication of the Bank. The Bank, with assets of $5 billion, is unquestionably wealthy. In addition, while the Bank's investment choices may have been unwise, its investment experience is extraordinary, and far surpasses most sophisticated individual investors. As a business entity, the Bank obviously has a business background, and its employees—hired for their business expertise—had extensive education and experience in economics and finance.

Despite its extensive investment experience and extraordinary resources, the Bank nevertheless contends that, while it may be sophisticated in certain types of investments, it was not sophisticated in CMO investments. *See, e.g., McAnally v. Gildersleeve,* 16 F.3d 1493, 1500 (8th Cir. 1994) (recognizing that an individual's sophistication in "stocks and bonds" did not necessarily suggest sophistication in commodities futures options); *Order Approving NASD Suitability Interpretation,* 61 Fed. Reg. 44,100, 44,112 (1996) (NASD Fair Practice Rules) (in approving NASD fair practice rules, SEC recognized that even a sophisticated institutional investor may not be capable of understanding a "particular investment risk"). The Bank argues that deposition testimony of its employees and an expert witness that the Bank was unsophisticated in CMO investments created a genuine issue of fact.

We reject this argument. The Bank's NNI unit, whose function was to invest Bank funds in dollar-denominated investments, employed three well-educated investment professionals to select a sound, but profitable, investment strategy. Mendez, Aguirre, and Buentello conducted a thorough, independent investigation of the benefits of risks of CMO investments by attending seminars, purchasing treatises on the subject, and developing a multi-step review process for each CMO investment. Rather than blindly relying on Epley and Alex. Brown, the record shows that the Bank rejected Epley's suggested investments far more often than it accepted them. Indeed, the Bank consulted with five other brokerage houses regarding CMO investments, and each of these brokerage houses gave the Bank detailed information describing the benefits and the risks of CMO investments. After a year of trading in CMOs, the Bank displayed a knowledge and an aggressiveness that belie its current claim that it did not understand CMO investments. See J.A. at 447-48 (indicating dramatic price changes over short time periods for many of the Bank's profitable CMO trades: FNMA 92 112 SC was sold after one day at a profit reflecting an annual increase of over 350 percent, FN 93-

115 SB was sold after two weeks at a profit reflecting an annual increase of around 58 percent; FNMA 1992 162 SB was sold after two weeks at a profit reflecting an annual increase of around 38 percent); NASD Fair Practice Rules, 61 Fed. Reg. at 44,105 n.20 ("[An institution] who initially needed help understanding a potential investment may ultimately develop an understanding and make an independent investment decision."). Accordingly, we agree with the district court that the Bank was a "sophisticated investor" for the purposes of this case. *See Banca Cremi v. Alex. Brown,* 955 F. Supp. 499, 515 (D. Md. 1997).

The second *Myers* factor also lends no support to the Bank's claim of justifiable reliance. There is no evidence in the record that the Bank enjoyed a long-standing business or personal relationship with Epley or Alex. Brown, and the undisputed evidence strongly supports the lack of any such relationship. The Bank began purchasing CMOs a mere two months after first being "cold called" by Epley, and the conduct of the Bank—consulting with competing brokerage houses and rejecting most of Epley's recommendations—suggests that the Bank dealt with Epley and Alex. Brown at arm's length. Accordingly, this is not a situation where the defendants could have exploited the business relationship [with the plaintiff] knowing that [the plaintiff] was not likely to investigate the merits of [the defendants'] recommendation." *Straub v. Vaisman & Co.,* 540 F.2d 591, 598 (3d Cir. 1976) (quotations omitted).

The third, fifth, and sixth *Myers* factors look to whether the Bank had access to the relevant information on CMOs, whether Epley and Alex. Brown concealed the alleged fraud, and whether the Bank had an opportunity to detect the fraud. In this case, there is no allegation that Apley or Alex. Brown concealed specific risks of individual investments, but rather that they misrepresented the risks associated with an entire field of investment. Clearly, the Bank—through its independent research, contacts with other brokerage houses, and discussions with Epley and Alex. Brown—not only had access to, but actually possessed more than sufficient information to make it aware of the substantial risks of investing in CMOs. The Bank knew that, although it could enjoy substantial earnings from CMO investments if interest rates decreased or remained the same, any increase in interest rates could wreak havoc on its CMO investment strategy. The Bank also knew that more sophisticated analyses of its CMO portfolio were available, such as the price analysis performed by Alex. Brown on the Bank's portfolio in July 1993. The July 1993 price analysis indicated that both inverse floaters and inverse IOs were more sensitive to interest rate increases than other types of CMOs, not to mention other more conservative fixed-rate investments such as U.S. Treasury Bonds. Despite possessing this information, the Bank purchased the six CMOs and never requested any analysis either before or after purchase.

The fourth *Myers* factor, whether the defendants owed a fiduciary duty to the plaintiff, is also not implicated in this case. As will be discussed below, Epley and Alex. Brown were not the agents of the Bank, but rather interacted with the Bank at arm's length in principal-to-principal dealings, and no common law fiduciary duty was ever created.

The seventh *Myers* factor looks to whether the Bank initiated or sought to expedite the transaction. While the Bank had sufficient time to review each of its CMO purchases, and evidenced independent decision-making by rejecting numerous suggested purchases by Epley and employing elaborate procedures to review each suggested purchase, it was Epley who initially suggested these investments to the Bank. Accordingly, we agree with the Bank that this factor lends some support to its argument for justifiable reliance. *But see Chance v. F.N. Wolf & Co.,* No. 93-2390, 1994 WL 529901, at *6 (4th Cir. Sept. 30, 1994) (unpublished, table decision reported at 36 F.3d 1091) (defendant entitled to judgment as a matter of law on justifiable reliance despite fact that defendant "initiated all of the stock transactions").

The final *Myers* factor looks to whether the misrepresentations were general or specific. The Bank argues, and we agree, that the defendants' alleged misstatements were general. Contrary to the Bank, however, we conclude that a general statement creates *less* justifiable reliance than would a specific statement. *See Hillson Partners Ltd. Partnership v. Adage Corp.,* 42 F.3d 204, 215 (4th Cir. 1994) (explaining that investor is more justified in relying on specific predictions); *Zobrist v. Coal-X, Inc.,* 708 F.2d 1511, 1518 (10th Cir. 1983) (noting that there is no "valid reason" to rely on general misrepresentations as to risk when more specific warnings have been provided); *Hughes v. Dempsey-Tegeler & Co.,* 534 F.2d 156, 177 (9th Cir. 1976) (sophisticated investor was not justified in relying on general positive comments regarding investment risks). Epley's general positive statements concerning CMOs did not justify reliance when the Bank possessed a variety of resources, including investment specific yield and average life tables, scholarly works, and an article published in a popular business journal explaining in great detail the workings and risks of CMOs.

In sum, in this case the Bank had access to an extraordinary wealth of information regarding CMOs. With few exceptions, the depth and breadth of this information illustrated one overriding point: investments in CMOs, while potentially very profitable, were undoubtedly highly risky. As a sophisticated business entity handling five billion dollars of other people's money, the Bank had the advice of its own employees and a horde of the defendants' competitors. Nevertheless, the Bank invested in CMOs through arm's length dealings with the defendants. While the vast majority of these investments were profitable for the Bank, a half-dozen proved disastrously timed, and the Bank now alleges that its misfortune resulted from its justifiable naivete in listening to the defendants' purported lies.

As in any "action[ ] for fraud, reliance on false statements must be accompanied by a right to rely." *Foremost Guar. Corp. v. Meritor Sav. Bank,* 910 F.2d 118, 125 (4th Cir. 1990). Here, the Bank lost its right to rely by its own recklessness. The Bank continued to purchase CMOs after it had sufficient information, given its sophistication, to be well apprised of the risks it would face were interest rates to rise. Given that the Bank was aware of the risks involved in investing in CMOs, the Bank was not justified in relying on Epley and Alex. Brown's alleged omissions and misstatements. Accordingly, we affirm the district court's grant of summary judgment against the Bank on this claim....

5. Price Protection: Markups and Other Matters

Page 1120. Add the following at the end of the carryover paragraph:

In *Banca Cremi v. Alex. Brown & Co.*, 132 F.3d 1017 (4th Cir. 1997), discussed in the previous section, the court also considered whether Alex. Brown committed fraud in not disclosing its mark-ups on the CMO interests it sold to the bank. Brown made over $2 million in mark-ups on sales of some $100 million in interests. Most of, though not all, the mark-ups were below the 5 percent "guideline." However, the bank offered expert testimony that in this setting, any mark-up of more than 1 percent was unreasonable. Expressing a good bit of discomfort with allowing such a case to go to trial given ease of making such a claim and the fact that the SEC has never chosen to mandate full disclosure of mark-ups, the court determined—based on the evidence available to it in considering defendant's motion—that the amount of the mark-up was completely unimportant to the bank. Its only interest was in its own cost. From this, the court concluded that there was no possible reliance on any "shingle theory" fair price representation.

Are you convinced? Had there been disclosure of an apparently sizeable mark-up, how would we know whether the bank would have acted differently? Would this case have been better decided on right to rely grounds?

17
The Investment Advisers and Investment Company Acts of 1940

B. Mutual Funds and Other Investment Companies

3. Sales and Redemptions of Mutual Fund Shares

b. Sales Literature and Advertising

Page 1179. At the end of the first full paragraph add the following:

In 1998, the SEC took a major step toward allowing mutual funds to be sold in a "user friendly" fashion by adopting Rule 498 under the '33 Act, which authorizes funds to utilize a "profile prospectus." This prospectus would be very brief compared to the normal disclosure, containing only the most important "highlight" information for potential investors. Investors could purchase mutual fund shares with this disclosure alone, receiving the full prospectus with their confirmation. At the same time, the Commission also simplified the full prospectus in Form N-1A. Securities Act Releases No. 7512-13, March 13, 1998. *Query:* If a profile prospectus works for mutual fund purchases, should the same idea be extended to IPOs and other public offerings by corporations generally?

||18||
Transnational Securities Fraud

A. The Extraterritorial Application of U.S. Securities Laws

1. In General

Page 1204. Insert the following case at the end of the section.

Kauthar SDN BHD v. Sternberg
149 F.3d 659 (7th Cir. 1998)

RIPPLE, CIRCUIT JUDGE. [T]his case centers on a $38 million investment made by Kauthar in a company called Rimsat, Ltd. Kauthar is a Malaysian corporation with its principal place of business in Kuala Lumpur, Malaysia. Rimsat, whose principal place of business is in Fort Wayne, Indiana, was incorporated in the Caribbean island nation of Nevis for the purpose of providing satellite communications services to customers within the Pacific Rim region. These satellite communications were to be provided using satellites that Rimsat had contracted to purchase from a Russian satellite company. The satellites were to be placed in geosynchronous (or geostationary) orbit positions ("GSOs") that were leased to Rimsat by a company called Friendly Islands Satellite Communications, Ltd., doing business as "Tongasat." Tongasat is incorporated in the Pacific Rim Kingdom of Tonga.

Apparently, there is a limited number of GSOs available in the world because satellites may not be put in too close a proximity to one another or else communications interference occurs. Satellites in geosynchronous orbit, by definition, stay essentially in the same spot over the earth and on the same equatorial plane. Consequently, the number of these spots in space is finite and, as with all scarce resources for which there is demand, they are valuable. The International Telecommunications Union ("ITU") and the International Frequency Registration Board, agencies of the United Nations, coordinate the registration and regulation of GSO positions. Only sovereign nations may apply to the ITU for rights to a GSO position for operation of a satellite. In this case, the Kingdom of Tonga obtained seven GSOs which it leased out to others through its company Tongasat. Rimsat's apparent plan was to make its fortune by buying relatively inexpensive Russian communications satellites, leasing GSOs from Tongasat and selling satellite communications services.

Not surprisingly, such a venture is highly capital-intensive. Rimsat and various of the individual defendants involved in forming Rimsat and Tongasat sought investors for this project. Kauthar allegedly was convinced, on the basis of various communications and meetings, that Rimsat was a worthy investment, and it sank $38 million into the venture through a purchase of Rimsat stock. Kauthar effected this purchase by wiring funds to Rimsat's bank in Fort Wayne, Indiana.

In January 1995, several of Rimsat's creditors forced Rimsat into bankruptcy by filing a petition for involuntary bankruptcy in . . . Indiana. Six weeks later, when Kauthar realized that its equity stake in Rimsat was worthless, it brought this suit. Essentially, Kauthar alleged in its complaint that all of the parties involved in soliciting its investment in Rimsat intentionally misled Kauthar about the investment. Kauthar specifically points to a document that it terms a "prospectus" that was disseminated by Rimsat to outline the company's investment and business plans. In its 113-page amended complaint, Kauthar identifies alleged misrepresentations contained in the prospectus in addition to other misrepresentations and omissions it alleges were made in the course of dealings. . . .

II

Discussion

A. Securities Fraud Claims

Kauthar alleged in Counts I and II of its complaint violations of § 10(b) of the 1934 Act and Rule 10b-5. . . . In Counts III and IV of its complaint, Kauthar alleged additional securities fraud claims predicated on violations of § 17(a) of the 1933 Act. Before we address the specifics of each claim, we first consider a problem common to all of them.

1. Extraterritorial Application of the Antifraud Securities Statutes

The district court determined that the securities violations alleged by Kauthar in Counts I-IV of its complaint were beyond the ambit of statutory protection because they involved transnational securities transactions without a sufficient connection to the United States. . . .

Courts have struggled for many years to define with meaningful precision the extent to which the antifraud provisions of the securities laws apply to securities transactions that are predominantly extraterritorial in nature but have some connection to the United States. The courts that have addressed the issue have noted that the question is a difficult one because Congress has given little meaningful guidance on the issue. In addition, resort to the legislative history of the securities acts does little to illuminate Congress' intent in this area. . . . In fact, some courts have admitted candidly that, in fashioning an approach to the issue of extraterritorial application of the securities laws, policy considerations and the courts' best judgment have been utilized to determine the reach of the federal securities laws.

In dealing with this difficult area we begin, as we always do in matters of statutory interpretation, with the words of the statute. Although the statutory language gives us little guidance, it does give us some clue of the direction we must take. Congress did leave some indication in the language of the securities laws about their intended application to foreign commerce. Section 10(b) prohibits fraud by the "use of any means or instrumentality of interstate commerce or of the mails" in "connection with the purchase or sale of any security." "Interstate commerce" is defined to include "trade, commerce, transportation, or communication . . . between any foreign country and any State." 15 U.S.C. § 78c(a)(17). A single passage in the statute addresses foreign transactions explicitly. . . . § 30(b) states that the 1934 Act "shall not apply to any person insofar as he transacts a business in securities without the jurisdiction of the United States, unless he transacts such business in contravention of such rules and regulations as the Commission may prescribe as necessary or appropriate to prevent the evasion of this chapter." 15 U.S.C. § 78dd(b). The Supreme Court has said that "it is a longstanding principle of American law 'that legislation of Congress, unless a contrary intent appears, is meant to apply only within the territorial jurisdiction of the United States.'" *EEOC v. Arabian Am. Oil Co.*, 499 U.S. 244, 248, 113 L. Ed. 2d 274, 111 S. Ct. 1227 (1991). . . . But, as some courts have noted, this statutory language suggests that the antifraud provisions were intended to apply to some transnational securities transactions.

Although the circuits that have confronted the matter seem to agree that there are some transnational situations to which the antifraud provisions of the securities laws are applicable, agreement appears to end at that point. Identification of those circumstances that warrant such regulation has produced a disparity in approach, to some degree doctrinal and to some degree attitudinal, as the courts have striven to implement, in Judge Friendly's words, "what Congress would have wished if these problems had occurred to it." *Bersch v. Drexel Firestone, Inc.*, 519 F.2d 974, 993 (2d Cir.), *cert. denied*, 423 U.S. 1018 (1975).

These efforts have produced two basic approaches to determining whether the transaction in question ought to be subject to American securities fraud regulation. These two approaches (we think that "test" is too inflexible a term to characterize the present state of the case law) focus on whether the activity in question has had a sufficient impact on or relation to the United States, its markets or its citizens to justify American regulation of the situation. Specifically, one approach focuses on the domestic conduct in question, and the other focuses on the domestic effects resulting from the transaction at issue.

When focusing on the effects, the courts seek to determine whether actions "occurring in foreign countries have caused foreseeable and substantial harm to interests in the United States." *Mak v. Wocom Commodities Ltd.*, 112 F.3d 287, 289 (7th Cir. 1997). . . . Several cases have examined the type and severity of the harm that must be suffered domestically in order to enable an exercise of jurisdiction. This case, however, affords us no occasion to explore this approach; the record does not reveal sufficient effect on domestic interests to justify its invocation here.

In contrast with the effects analysis, which examines actions occurring outside of the United States, the conduct analysis focuses on actions occurring in this country as they "relate[ ] to the alleged scheme to defraud." *Tamari*, 730 F.2d at 1107. The chronic difficulty with such a methodology has been describing, in sufficiently precise terms, the sort of conduct occurring in the United States that ought to be adequate to trigger American regulation of the transaction. Indeed, the circuits that have confronted the matter have articulated a number of methodologies.

The predominant difference among the circuits, it appears, is the degree to which the American-based conduct must be related causally to the fraud and the resultant harm to justify the application of American securities law. At one end of the spectrum, the District of Columbia Circuit appears to require that the domestic conduct at issue must itself constitute a securities violation. *See Zoelsch*, 824 F.2d at 31 ("Jurisdiction will lie in American courts where the domestic conduct comprises all the elements

■ ❙ 18. Transnational Securities Fraud   Page 1204. ❙ ■

of a defendant's conduct necessary to establish a violation of section 10(b) and Rule 10b-5.").[10] At the other end of the spectrum, the Third, Eighth and Ninth Circuits, although also focusing on whether the United States-based conduct caused the plaintiffs' loss, to use the Fifth Circuit's words, "generally require some lesser quantum of conduct." *Robinson v. TCI/US West Communications, Inc.*, 117 F.3d 900, 906 (5th Cir. 1997). *In SEC v. Kasser*, 548 F.2d 109, 114 (3d Cir.), *cert. denied*, 431 U.S. 938 (1977), the Third Circuit stated that the conduct came within the scope of the statute if "at least some activity designed to further a fraudulent scheme occurs within this country." The Eighth Circuit, in *Continental Grain (Australia) Pty. Ltd. v. Pacific Oilseeds, Inc.*, 592 F.2d 409, 421 (8th Cir. 1979), held that the antifraud provisions were applicable when the domestic conduct "was in furtherance of a fraudulent scheme and was significant with respect to its accomplishment." The Ninth Circuit adopted the *Continental Grain* approach in *Grunenthal GmbH v. Hotz*, 712 F.2d 421, 425 (9th Cir. 1983).

Our colleagues in the Second and Fifth Circuits have set a course between the two extremes that we have just discussed. That approach requires a higher quantum of domestic conduct than do the Third, Eighth and Ninth Circuits. *See Robinson*, 117 F.3d 900, 905-06 (5th Cir. 1997). The Second Circuit has stated that foreign plaintiffs' suits under the antifraud provisions of the securities laws, such as *Kauthar*'s, will be "heard only when substantial acts in furtherance of the fraud were committed within the United States." *Psimenos v. E.F. Hutton & Co., Inc.*, 722 F.2d 1041, 1045 (2d Cir. 1983).[12] Furthermore, if the United States-based activities were merely

---

10. Indeed, in *Zoelsch*, the court expressed doubt "that an American court should ever assert jurisdiction over domestic conduct that causes loss to foreign investors." 824 F.2d at 32. In adopting this restrictive approach, the District of Columbia Circuit claimed to adopt expressly the Second Circuit's methodology. *See* id. at 33. We share the reservations of the Fifth Circuit as to whether the District of Columbia Circuit accurately portrayed the Second Circuit's jurisprudence. *See Robinson*, 117 F.3d at 905 n.10. Rather, we believe that the Fifth Circuit more accurately mirrored the Second Circuit's approach, which it articulated as: "Where (as here) the alleged fraud is in connection with a sale of securities to a foreigner outside the United States, the federal securities laws apply only if acts or culpable failures to act within the United States directly caused the plaintiff's loss." *Robinson*, 117 F.3d at 905.

12. In *Psimenos*, a case brought under the Commodity Exchange Act, the Greek plaintiff alleged fraud in the defendant's manager's handling of his commodities transactions. Although the court noted that "most of the fraudulent misrepresentations alleged in the complaint occurred outside the United States," it found the conduct analysis was satisfied because a pamphlet emanating from the defendant's New York office indicated that the managers would be supervised and because the alleged fraud was completed "by trading domestic futures contracts on American commodities exchanges." 722 F.2d at 1044, 1046. Other cases have indicated that effecting transactions on exchanges in America is sufficient conduct in the United

preparatory in nature, or if the " 'bulk of the activity was performed in foreign countries,' " jurisdiction will not exist. Id. at 1046 (quoting *IIT v. Vencap, Ltd.*, 519 F.2d 1001, 1018 (2d Cir. 1975)). In addition, only "where conduct 'within the United States directly caused' the loss will a district court have jurisdiction over suits by foreigners who have lost money through sales abroad." Id. (quoting *Bersch v. Drexel Firestone, Inc.*, 519 F.2d 974, 993 (2d Cir.)).

Although this court has not had occasion to articulate an approach to the extraterritorial application of the securities laws, we have employed these concepts with respect to analogous actions brought under the Commodity Exchange Act. *See Mak*, 112 F.3d at 288-89; *Tamari*, 730 F.2d at 1107 & n.11. In that context, we have stated that "when the conduct occurring in the United States is material to the successful completion of the alleged scheme, jurisdiction is asserted based on the theory that Congress would not have intended the United States to be used as a base for effectuating the fraudulent conduct of foreign companies." *Tamari*, 730 F.2d at 1108. We think that our approach under the Commodities Act ought to be followed with respect to the securities laws and, although stated more generally, that it represents the same midground as that identified by the Second and Fifth Circuits. In our view, the absence of all but the most rudimentary Congressional guidance counsels that federal courts should be cautious in determining that transnational securities matters are within the ambit of our antifraud statutes. Nevertheless, we would do serious violence to the policies of these statutes if we did not recognize our Country's manifest interest in ensuring that the United States is not used as a "base of operations" from which to "defraud foreign securities purchasers or sellers." *Kasser*, 548 F.2d at 116. This interest is amplified by the fact that we live in an increasingly global financial community. The Second and Fifth Circuit's iterations of the test embody a satisfactory balance of these competing considerations. This analytical pattern will enable the courts to address situations in which the United States is being used as a launching pad for fraudulent international securities schemes. At the same time, it will cause us to refrain from adjudicating disputes which have little in the way of a significant connection to the United States.

We believe, therefore, that federal courts have jurisdiction over an alleged violation of the antifraud provisions of the securities laws when the conduct occurring in the United States directly causes the plaintiff's alleged loss in that the conduct forms a substantial part of the alleged fraud and is material to its success. This conduct must be more than merely prepara-

---

States to satisfy the conduct test. *See, e.g., Tamari*, 730 F.2d at 1108 (adopting district court's analysis that wiring of orders for commodity transactions to the United States and execution of those orders on Chicago exchanges was sufficient conduct to satisfy the conduct test).

tory in nature; however, we do not go so far as to require that the conduct occurring domestically must itself satisfy the elements of a securities violation.

We turn now to an application of these principles to Kauthar's allegations. Kauthar argues that a host of alleged general activities undertaken by various of the defendants constitutes conduct that was part of the scheme to defraud Kauthar and to solicit Kauthar's investment in Rimsat. Kauthar alleges that various documents containing fraudulent misrepresentations and omissions were prepared in the United States and were sent to it by wire and by the United States mail in an effort to obtain Kauthar's investment. Kauthar also alleges that phone calls were made from Fort Wayne, Indiana, and from San Diego, California, for the same purpose. Kauthar further alleges that the defendants had meetings and phone conversations in the United States to discuss the deceptive information contained in the prospectus and to "ultimately agree upon a plan to obtain equity funding from Kauthar by means of false and deceptive statements of fact." Thus, according to the complaint, the United States was utilized as a base of operations from which to launch the defendants' fraudulent scheme to defraud Kauthar. Moreover, Kauthar also alleges a set of specific acts that, in combination with those already mentioned, satisfy the conduct analysis. Specifically, Kauthar alleges that it wired the payment for the Rimsat securities, over $38 million, in six installments to Rimsat's bank account in Fort Wayne, Indiana. Therefore, Kauthar has alleged that the defendants conceived and planned a scheme to defraud Kauthar in the United States, that they prepared materials in support of the scheme to solicit the payment in the United States and sent those materials from the United States via the United States mail, and that they received in the United States the fraudulently solicited payment for the securities—the final step in the alleged fraud. We think these allegations sufficient to bring the alleged conduct within the ambit of the securities laws. . . .

3. Jurisdiction Based in Whole, or in Part, upon Conduct

Page 1216. Insert the following case immediately prior to the Notes and Questions.

Europe and Overseas Commodity Traders, S.A., v. Banque Paribas London
147 F.3d 118 (2d Cir. 1998)

OAKES, SENIOR CIRCUIT JUDGE: [T]he transaction underlying this dispute is entirely foreign inasmuch as there is no U.S. party, but not, strictly speaking, wholly extraterritorial in that [Europe and Overseas Commodity Traders, S.A. (EOC), a Panamanian corporation] alleges that an offer to sell foreign securities was made over the telephone and facsimile to its sole shareholder and agent, Alan Carr, who was in Florida, and both parties agree that orders to purchase securities were placed from Florida. We therefore address the question whether phone calls and facsimiles to a person on U.S. soil provide enough of a connection to the United States to implicate the registration and fraud provisions of U.S. securities laws, and give us jurisdiction thereunder. . . .

I

Facts

. . . EOC's account at [Banque Paribas, a French Bank] was established in London in 1992. The "Non-discretionary Investment Agreement" between EOC and Paribas was executed on October 22, 1992. . . . In this agreement, EOC gave a corporate registration address in Panama and a mailing address in Monaco. . . .

In October of 1993, Carr was visiting England, as he often does in the autumn. Arida [a U.K. national who works as an account manager in the London, England, office of Paribas], on October 7, there informed him that a substantial amount of cash had accumulated in EOC's account, and offered to recommend an attractive investment opportunity for the money. Carr says he expressed interest in the proposal, but explained to Arida that he was preparing to leave for Florida on the 9th and that he would be happy to hear more after his arrival.

In a series of telephone conversations which began on October 14, Carr and Arida resumed their discussion of EOC's investment in the Fund as planned after Carr's arrival in Florida. The parties agree that each party initiated at least some of these calls. Carr claims that these conversations with Arida were their first significant discussion of the Paribas Global Bond Futures Fund, S.A. (the "Fund"). Carr also alleges that Arida misled him by conveying the following facts, which EOC now claims are not accurate: (a) the Fund was overseen by Paribas's proprietary trading desk; (b) the investors' capital in the Fund was traded along with Paribas's own capital; and (c) the Fund traded securities based primarily on technical as opposed to fundamental considerations. In reliance on these statements, Carr says that from Florida he ordered EOC's first purchase of shares of the Fund on October 18, 1993. He also alleges that these representations were repeated on the occasion of each of his subsequent six purchases which, together with the October 18 purchase, totaled some $1,800,000. . . .

Arida disputes this version of the events. He claims that his first significant conversation with Carr about the Fund occurred while Carr was still in England. He also asserts that Carr ordered the first purchase of Fund shares from England. . . .

The district court found . . . that plaintiff EOC's principal place of business was in Monaco, and that the initial purchase of Fund shares occurred on October 8, 1993, a date when both parties agree Carr was still in England. The court also relied on the sworn statement of Corbiau, Secretary of the Fund that "insofar as I am aware, no investor in the Fund is a U.S. citizen or resident." . . . We do not think that the district court needed to conclude, contrary to plaintiff's assertions, that . . . the plaintiff's principal place of business was in Monaco. We think that it could have based its holding only on findings that EOC . . . made such representations to Paribas, and, thus, Paribas reasonably trusted that at all times during these transactions the bank was dealing with a Panamanian corporation with offices in Monaco.

For reasons discussed next, even accepting as true EOC's allegations that the initial offer to sell Fund shares occurred while Carr was in Florida, the transactions between EOC and Paribas did not implicate the prescriptive jurisdiction of the federal securities laws.

II

Discussion

Appellant EOC emphasizes in its briefs to this court that the district court did not discuss the claims at the heart of this case: sale of unregistered securities of an unregistered investment company to an individual on U.S. soil in violation of §§ 5 and 12 of the Securities Act of 1933. . . .

A. Registration under the 1933 Act.

EOC claims that the same "conduct and effects test," which this circuit applies to determine the extraterritorial scope of the fraud provisions of the federal securities laws, should be applied to determine the appropriate reach of the federal registration requirements. The relevant "conduct," EOC maintains, was the solicitation and sale of unregistered securities in the United States, and the relevant "effect" was the consummation of the sale of unregistered securities to a person within the United States. In other words, EOC appears to argue that any solicitation of unregistered securities within the territory of the United States is within the scope of the registration laws, and thus forbidden, without regard to the identity or nationality of any party.

The decided law of this circuit clearly states that the antifraud provisions may reach certain transactions not within the registration requirements of our securities law. *Consolidated Gold Fields PLC v. Minorco, S.A.*, 871 F.2d 252, 262 (2d Cir. 1989) ("As we observed in Bersch ... the antifraud provisions of American securities laws have broader extraterritorial reach than American filing requirements."); *see also Bersch*, 519 F.2d at 986 ("It is elementary that the anti-fraud provisions of the federal securities laws apply to many transactions which are neither within the registration requirements nor on organized American markets.") We therefore reject EOC's assertion that the "same standard" applies to the antifraud and registration laws, if EOC means that the registration and fraud provisions are coextensive. The analysis of jurisdiction to prescribe rules governing foreign transactions is guided by "the nature and source of the claim asserted." *See Zoelsch v. Arthur Andersen & Co.*, 262 U.S. App. D.C. 300, 824 F.2d 27, 33 n.4 (D.C. Cir. 1987) (comparing the role of the underlying claim in subject matter jurisdiction analysis to that in other "threshold issues" such as standing).

In contrast to the antifraud provisions of the 1934 Act, the SEC has provided some guidance as to the applicability of registration requirement of the 1933 Act to foreign transactions. We turn first to this regulation. However, we acknowledge that our precedent determining the extraterritorial reach of related provisions of the U.S. securities laws may provide some assistance in filling any gaps in the SEC's treatment of the scope of the registration provisions.

Under Regulation S, which was issued by the SEC ..., there are two ways that a sale of securities could fall outside § 5's registration requirement. First, a transaction could be "outside the United States," and, second, it could fall into either one of two exceptions defined by the SEC.... Regulation S adopts a "territorial approach" to § 5. The two so-called "safe harbor" exemptions permit the issuance and resale of securities under certain specified conditions. Offerings and resales meeting these conditions are deemed to take place outside the United States for the purpose of § 5.

We first examine the safe harbors to determine if either one clearly applies to this transaction. The issuer safe harbor appears to be the only exemption plausibly available to the Fund. ... Two general conditions, however, must be met for either of the safe harbors to apply: first, no "directed selling efforts" may be made in the United States. The release defines "directed selling efforts" as marketing efforts such as mailings or seminars in the United States designed to induce the purchase of securities purportedly being distributed abroad. Second, any offer or sale must fit the definition of an "offshore transaction," which requires inter alia that no offer be made to a person in the United States.

Given the facts alleged by EOC in this case, we cannot say that the

Fund can clearly rely on the issuer's safe harbor. EOC says that Arida's representations made over the telephone and facsimile to Carr in Florida resulted in his entering a purchase order on behalf of EOC. This alleged conduct could qualify as either "directed selling efforts" or a forbidden offer to a person in the United States. . . .

A transaction not within either of the safe harbors may still be outside of the United States within the meaning of 17 C.F.R. § 230.901. . . .

Our research has uncovered no case or decision of the SEC construing §230.901 with respect to transients visiting the United States, so we work on an essentially blank slate.

We believe that the conduct and effects test used to determine the reach of the anti-fraud provisions of U.S. securities laws can be adapted to analyze what is outside the specific safe harbors yet still "outside the United States" under Regulation S. The conduct and effects test was developed by the courts in the absence of clear Congressional guidance as to the jurisdictional reach of the antifraud provisions of the securities laws. . . . The antifraud provisions are designed to remedy deceptive and manipulative conduct with the potential to harm the public interest or the interests of investors. . . . In outlining the extraterritorial reach of these provisions, courts have reasoned that Congress would not want the United States to become a base for fraudulent activity harming foreign investors, or "conduct," see *Psimenos v. E.F. Hutton & Co.*, 722 F.2d 1041, 1045 (2d Cir. 1983), and that Congress would want to redress harms perpetrated abroad which have a substantial impact on investors or markets within the United States, or "effects." See *Schoenbaum*, 405 F.2d at 206; *Consolidated Gold Fields*, 871 F.2d at 261-62. However, because it is well-settled in this Circuit that "the anti-fraud provisions of American securities laws have broader extraterritorial reach than American filing requirements," id. at 262, the extent of conduct or effect in the United States needed to invoke U.S. jurisdiction over a claimed violation of the registration provisions must be greater than that which would trigger U.S. jurisdiction over a claim of fraud. To adapt the conduct and effects test for use in interpreting the registration provisions, we must take into account Congress's distinct purpose in drafting the registration laws.

Congress passed the registration provisions "to assure full and fair disclosure in connection with the public distribution of securities." James D. Cox et al., Securities Regulation 45 (1991). Through mandatory disclosure, Congress sought to promote informed investing and to deter the kind of fraudulent salesmanship that was believed to have led to the market collapse of 1929. Id. at 14 (citing H.R. Rep. No. 85 (1933)). The registration provisions are thus prophylactic in nature. Seen in this light, the registration provisions also can be said to aim at certain conduct with the potential for discernible effects. Specifically, the registration provisions are designed to prevent the offer of securities in the United States securities market without accompanying standardized disclosures to aid investors, a course of conduct. This conduct, in turn, has the effect of creating interest in and demand for unregistered securities. To avoid this result, in keeping with Congress's purpose, the registration provisions should apply to those offers of unregistered securities that tend to have the effect of creating a market for unregistered securities in the United States; and by "creating a market" we do not mean to imply that the conduct must be directed at a large number of people.

The Commissioner's release accompanying Regulation S, as well as the early version of Regulation S, support the application of this conduct and effects test. The factors originally listed in Regulation S pertaining to when an offer or sale of a security occurs outside the United States largely pertain to efforts to create a market in the United States for unregistered foreign securities. These factors were "the locus of the offer or sale, the absence of directed selling efforts in the United States, and the justified expectation of the parties to the transaction as to the applicability of the registration requirements of the U.S. securities laws." Offshore Offers and Sales, Securities Act Release No. 33-6779, 53 Fed. Reg. 22661, 22661-2 (proposed June 17, 1988). Such a test is also consistent with earlier statements by the SEC about the scope of the registration provisions. *See, e.g.*, SEC Release No. 33-6863, 55 Fed. Reg. at 18308 ("The Commission, however, historically has recognized that registration of offerings with only incidental jurisdictional contacts should not be required."). . . .

The nearly de minimis U.S. interest in the transactions presented in the instant case precludes our finding that U.S. jurisdiction exists under the more limited conduct and effect standard appropriate under the registration provisions of the 1933 Act. Under the facts as alleged by EOC, there was conduct in the United States because Arida called Carr here and Carr executed his order here. However, the conduct was not such as to have the effect of creating a market for those securities in the United States. Carr's presence here was entirely fortuitous and personal, and the actual purchaser of shares in the Fund was an offshore corporation without a place of business here.[8]

Although the offer or sale of an unregistered security to an agent of a foreign company in the United States may in some cases tend to create a market for the security in the United States, this is not such a case. EOC was conducting no business in the United States through Carr, nor

---

8. While my colleagues do not agree, the author of this opinion would add that:

> Having chosen to do business through an offshore corporation to avoid taxes and other regulatory burdens, Carr cannot now claim to be an alter ego of EOC. *See* Carey v. National Oil Corp., 592 F.2d 673, 676 (2d Cir. 1979) ("We will not 'pierce the corporate veil' in favor of those who created it.").

otherwise benefiting from his presence here. Nor did the transaction involve a U.S. broker or other U.S. financial entity. Arida, on his part, did nothing to encourage a market for securities in the United States. He made no calls or solicitations to individuals he had reason to suspect were American citizens or permanent residents in the United States, and he directed no general sales efforts here. Accordingly, we hold that the securities sold to EOC did not fall under the registration requirements of the 1933 Act, and that we therefore lack subject matter jurisdiction over EOC's § 5 claims.

Of course, we do not attempt in ruling on this case to provide a set of definitive rules togovern future transactions. Nor do we mean to suggest that standards developed under the anti-fraud provisions may be incorporated wholesale into the registration context. The exact contours of the conduct and effects test, as applied to registration cases, must remain to be defined on a case-by-case basis. . . .

C. Antifraud Provisions.

As discussed above, the antifraud provisions of the securities laws have been held to reach beyond the registration requirement of the 1933 Act. Our conclusion with respect to registration does not therefore eliminate the possibility that jurisdiction could be found under § 10(b) of the 1934 Act and Rule 10b-5. Congress's power to impose civil penalties for fraud in predominately foreign securities transactions is limited only by the Due Process Clause of the Fifth Amendment. In a long line of decisions stretching back to *Schoenbaum*, this circuit has recognized that the federal securities laws do not reach this constitutional limit. We have looked for conduct, *see, e.g., Leasco,* 468 F.2d at 133-34; effects, *see, e.g., Schoenbaum,* 405 F.2d at 206-09; or a combination thereof, *see, e.g., Itoba,* 54 F.3d at 122, in the United States to arrive at "our best judgment as to what Congress would have wished if these problems [of extraterritorial application] had occurred to it." *Bersch,* 519 F.2d at 993 (footnote omitted).

Perhaps the most difficult cases under the conduct test have concerned activity in the United States that causes, or plays a substantial part in causing, harm to foreign interests overseas. By contrast, as stated above, the effects test concerns the impact of overseas activity on U.S. investors and securities traded on U.S. securities exchanges.[12] Telephone calls and facsimile trans-

---

12. As formulated in Bersch, the effects test concerns sales to "Americans resident in the United States." 519 F.2d at 993. We agree with the opinion expressed by Judge Motley in O'Driscoll v. Merrill Lynch, Pierce, Fenner & Smith, Inc., 1983 U.S. Dist. LEXIS 13984, 1983 WL 1360, *3 (S.D.N.Y. Sept. 8, 1983) that "the United States would have a greater interest in protecting foreigners residing within its borders than foreigners resident abroad" and that, for this reason, U.S. residence of individual investors—not American nationality—must be the focus of the effects test. *See* Restatement of Foreign Relations § 416 (1)(a)(ii) (1987) ("The United States may generally exercise jurisdiction . . . with respect to . . . any offer to enter

■| Page 1216.　　　　　　　　18. Transnational Securities Fraud |■

missions conveying offers to sell securities and investment information could be characterized as either conduct or effects in the United States.

If evaluated as an effect, the U.S. interest affected by this transaction is indiscernible for reasons already discussed: the plaintiff is a Panamanian corporation; the individual who placed the purchase orders, and who ultimately suffered any losses, is a Canadian citizen; the securities are not traded on a U.S. exchange; and no effect on a U.S. affiliated company is alleged by EOC. There is, thus, no U.S. entity that Congress could have wished to protect from the machinations of swindlers. . . .

The analysis becomes somewhat more difficult when we turn to the conduct test. The conduct test in this circuit has been stated in two parts as follows:

> the anti-fraud provisions of the federal securities laws . . . apply to losses from sales of securities to Americans resident abroad if, but only if, acts (or culpable failures to act) of material importance in the United States have significantly contributed thereto; but . . . do not apply to losses from sales of securities to foreigners outside the United States unless acts (or culpable failures to act) within the United States directly caused such losses.

Bersch, 519 F.2d at 993. Or, alternatively, we have said more simply that activity in the United States that is "merely preparatory" to a securities fraud elsewhere will not implicate our antifraud laws. *Itoba*, 54 F.3d at 122 (citing *Bersch*). EOC's allegations do not fit neatly into either of the two categories outlined in *Bersch*. Clearly, EOC is not a U.S. entity: even were we to look through the Panamanian corporate identity, its owner, a Canadian citizen, is still foreign. Yet, on the other hand, EOC alleges solicitation and sale of securities within the United States, and the second *Bersch* category is specifically limited to sales outside the United States. EOC's claim, thus, falls in yet another category which, although identified, was not addressed in *Bersch*: "losses to foreigners from sales to them within the United States." 519 F.2d at 993. EOC's is a novel factual pattern not squarely governed by any of our decisions to date.

The facts alleged by EOC, nonetheless, satisfy the requirement that U.S. activity directly cause the harm to the foreign interest, which has in the past been the key element of litigation involving the conduct test.

---

into a securities transaction, made in the United States by or to a national or resident of the United States.") Indeed, as Judge Motley noted, *O'Driscoll*, 1983 U.S. Dist. LEXIS 13984, 1983 WL at *4, since alienage is a protected class under the Constitution, Graham v. Richardson, 403 U.S. 365, 91 S. Ct. 1848, 29 L. Ed. 2d 534 (1971), limiting the effects test to citizen investors would be constitutionally suspect. Plaintiff EOC is, however, a foreign corporation, and even Carr was only vacationing in the United States. We see no reason that the U.S. interest in protecting transients, who benefit from the protection of their own national governments, should be as great as that in protecting resident aliens.

Or, stated in the alternative language we have sometimes used, Arida's communications into the United States were more than "mere preparation" for the fraud. EOC alleges that Arida solicited, offered to sell, and accepted a purchase order for securities from Carr when he was in Florida. Carr also says he relied upon the allegedly misleading information given to him from abroad while he was present in the United States, and such reliance was the direct cause of the loss sustained by EOC. *Cf. Fidenas*, 606 F.2d 5 (all parties were foreign, and this court declined jurisdiction because conduct in the United States was secondary or ancillary to the alleged fraud). The difficult question raised by EOC's allegations is whether Arida's communications to Carr in Florida may be considered activity within the United States for the purpose of the antifraud provisions of the security laws sufficient to support the jurisdiction of this court under the 1934 Act. We believe that they were not.

Although phone calls (or any other communications into the United States) soliciting or conveying an offer to sell securities ordinarily would be sufficient to support jurisdiction, it would be inconsistent with the law of this circuit to accept jurisdiction over this dispute, because the surrounding circumstances show that no relevant interest of the United States was implicated. In other words, a series of calls to a transient foreign national in the United States is not enough to establish jurisdiction under the conduct test without some additional factor tipping the scales in favor of our jurisdiction. Without such added weight, the exercise of prescriptive jurisdiction by Congress would be unreasonable . . . , and is particularly so when the transaction is clearly subject to the regulatory jurisdiction of another country with a clear and strong interest in redressing any wrong. We do not think Congress intended to make the securities laws have such a broad reach or to make U.S. courts available for such suits.

In the past, we have found jurisdiction over a predominantly foreign securities transaction under the conduct test when, in addition to communications with or meetings in the United States, there has also been a transaction on a U.S. exchange, economic activity in the U.S., harm to a U.S. party, or activity by a U.S. person or entity meriting redress. All of these factors are absent from EOC's allegations. *AVC Nederland B.V. v. Atrium Inv. Partnership*, 740 F.2d 148 (2d Cir. 1984), which Judge Friendly indicated was a very close case, id. at 154, provides the strongest support of EOC's position, but does not go far enough. *Nederland* concerned the sale of an interest in a partnership formed by Dutch nationals for the purpose of investing in U.S. real estate. Plaintiff-purchaser was also Dutch. Much of the negotiation during which the alleged misrepresentations were made occurred in the United States, but the deal was concluded abroad. Even though the consummation of the allegedly fraud-tainted sale occurred outside the United States, Judge Friendly's opinion found jurisdiction, after considering the many factors listed in § 403(2) of Tentative Draft No.2 of

■ | Page 1216.   18.   Transnational Securities Fraud | ■

the current Restatement. Specifically, the opinion found the extent of the activity within the regulating state and the economic activity connecting both the plaintiff and defendants to the United States weighed in favor of jurisdiction. Presumably, although the opinion does not say as much, it considered the U.S. real estate investments, which were the purpose of the partnership and the subject of the alleged fraud, to be economic activity connecting the parties to the United States within the meaning of § 403(2)(b) of the Tentative Draft. In any event, we find *Nederland* distinguishable for this reason. The sales by Paribas to EOC have no similar connection to the United States: EOC invested in Europe; and Paribas's offices in and any other connections to the United States have no relevance to these transactions. We therefore find that the slight additional factor of economic activity in the United States, which "tipped the balance" in favor of jurisdiction in *Nederland*, is absent from EOC's case.

In this case, there is no U.S. party to protect or punish, despite the fact that the most important piece of the alleged fraud—reliance on a misrepresentation—may have taken place in this country. Congress may not be presumed to have prescribed rules governing activity with strong connections to another country, if the exercise of such jurisdiction would be unreasonable in the light of established principles of U.S. and international law. See Restatement § 403. And, the answer to the question of what jurisdiction is reasonable depends in part on the regulated subject matter. Id. cmt. c. ("Regulation by the United States of the labor relations of a foreign vessel that regularly calls on the United States may be unreasonable; regulation of the vessel's safety standards may not be unreasonable.")

This case illustrates the kind of circumstances in which it is unreasonable to prescribe rules of conduct with respect to securities fraud, even when a misrepresentation is made in the United States and reliance occurs on U.S. soil. Section 10(b), although it sounds in the common law tort of fraud, is part of a regulatory system that serves the public interest of the United States in much the same way as banking and currency regulations. This apparent purpose of protecting and regulating an entire system led this court to extend, through the use of the effects test, the antifraud provisions of these laws to activity not ordinarily within the "presumptive" scope of legislation. *See Equal Employ. Opp. Comm'n v. Arabian American Oil Co.*, 499 U.S. 244, 248 111 S. Ct. 1227, 1230, 113 L. Ed. 2d 274 (1991) (legislation presumptively territorial); *Zoelsch*, 824 F.2d at 31 (same) (collecting cases).[19] The very considerations that have led this court to conclude

---

19. After adopting the Second Circuit's "conduct" test for the extraterritorial application of U.S. securities fraud laws, Judge Bork's opinion in *Zoelsch* noted "the test we adopt here does provide jurisdiction whenever any individual is defrauded in this country, regardless of whether the offer originates somewhere else, for the actual consummation of securities fraud in the United States in and of itself would constitute domestic conduct that satisfies all the elements of liability." *Zoelsch*, 824

that Congress meant for the securities antifraud laws to reach beyond our shores to certain fraudulent activities abroad militate against finding subject matter jurisdiction over EOC's complaint. It would be ironic if a foreign party seeking redress in a U.S. court could sidestep the effect requirement by stretching our notions of conduct in the United States to include telephone calls from abroad to an agent/owner of that party here fortuitously. The situation is entirely different from the difficult cases under the conduct test in which a U.S. person or entity is the source of misleading information causing harm elsewhere. The U.S. interest in punishing an English malfeasor working at a French bank branch in London who caused no harm here is not apparent. We therefore hold that the alleged solicitation, offer to sell, and purchases occurring while Carr was present in Florida did not bring this otherwise entirely foreign transaction within the antifraud provisions of U.S. securities law.

Conclusion

The decision of the district court dismissing plaintiff EOC's complaint for lack of subject matter jurisdiction is affirmed.

F.2d at 33 n.4. We agree with this general statement, but think it inapplicable when, as here, there is no U.S. citizen, resident or other identifiable U.S. interest concerned.